Arthurian Romance

Blackwell Introductions to Literature

This series sets out to provide concise and stimulating introductions to literary subjects. It offers books on major authors (from John Milton to James Joyce), as well as key periods and movements (from Old English literature to the contemporary). Coverage is also afforded to such specific topics as 'Arthurian Romance'. All are written by outstanding scholars as texts to inspire newcomers and others: non-specialists wishing to revisit a topic, or general readers. The prospective overall aim is to ground and prepare students and readers of whatever kind in their pursuit of wider reading.

Published

1. *John Milton* — Roy Flannagan
2. *Chaucer and the Canterbury Tales* — John Hirsh
3. *Arthurian Romance* — Derek Pearsall
4. *James Joyce* — Michael Seidel
5. *Mark Twain* — Stephen Railton
6. *The Modern Novel* — Jesse Matz
7. *Old Norse-Icelandic Literature* — Heather O'Donoghue
8. *Old English Literature* — Daniel Donoghue
9. *Modernism* — David Ayers
10. *Latin American Fiction* — Philip Swanson

Forthcoming

English Renaissance Literature — Michael Hattaway
American Literature and Culture 1900–1960 — Gail McDonald
Middle English — Thorlac Turville-Petre
Medieval Literature — David Wallace

Arthurian Romance

A Short Introduction

Derek Pearsall

Blackwell
Publishing

BLACKWELL PUBLISHING
350 Main Street, Malden, MA 02148-5020, USA
9600 Garsington Road, Oxford OX4 2DQ, UK
550 Swanston Street, Carlton, Victoria 3053, Australia

First published 2003 by Blackwell Publishing Ltd

9   2011

Library of Congress Cataloging-in-Publication Data

Pearsall, Derek Albert.
   Arthurian romance : a short introduction / Derek Pearsall.
      p. cm. — (Blackwell introduction to literature)
   Includes bibliographical references and index.
   ISBN 978-0-6312-3319-0 (alk. paper) — ISBN 978-0-6312-3320-6 (pbk. : alk. paper)
   1. Arthurian romances–History and criticism. I. Title. II. Series.

PN685 .P43 2003
809'.93351—dc21

                                        2002038486

A catalogue record for this title is available from the British Library.

Set in 10/13 pt Meridian
by Graphicraft Ltd, Hong Kong
Printed and bound in Malaysia
by Vivar Printing Sdn Bhd

The publisher's policy is to use permanent paper from mills that operate a sustainable
forestry policy, and which has been manufactured from pulp processed using acid-free and
elementary chlorine-free practices. Furthermore, the publisher ensures that the text paper
and cover board used have met acceptable environmental accreditation standards.

For further information on
Blackwell Publishing, visit our website:
www.blackwellpublishing.com

Contents

Preface

This book is a study of Arthurian romance, principally in English, from the beginnings to modern times. It is designed to accommodate the interests of new readers and old readers, of Arthurian enthusiasts and sceptics alike. It will consist chiefly of readings of the great works of Arthurian romance, from Chrétien de Troyes and Gottfried von Strassburg through Malory to Tennyson and beyond, the non-English works being treated in English translation. The representation of Arthurian themes in the pictorial arts and in other forms of visual medium will be part of the story. The readings will trace the fortunes of Arthur, Guenevere and Lancelot, and of Gawain, Tristan and the other knights of the Round Table, at the hands of different writers and artists throughout their life in literature and art. The attempt will be to show how the story has been the embodiment at different times of chivalric idealism, patriotic nationalism, spiritual aspiration, the idealization of romantic sexual love, and the fear of sexuality – and the critical and ironic questioning of all those forms of value; how romance was founded in epic and was at times metamorphosed in ballad, drama, elegy, satire and burlesque; how the Arthurian story, in all its manifestations, has provided a medium through which different cultures could express their deepest hopes and aspirations and contain and circumscribe their deepest fears and anxieties.

The book will begin with the early British treatments of the whole Arthurian story, in Geoffrey of Monmouth, Wace and Layamon, and pass on to the development of European Arthurian romance in the narratives (in French, German and English) of the lives, loves and exploits of Lancelot, Gawain, Tristan and Perceval, and the climax of these developments in the *Morte D'Arthur* of Sir Thomas Malory. It will continue with the breaking of the long 'Arthurian sleep' of the seventeenth and eighteenth centuries in the Romantic Revival and Tennyson's *Idylls of the King*, and conclude with the anti-Arthurian reaction of Mark Twain and the continuing extraordinary popularity of Arthurian romance and legend in modern fantasy-historical novels and children's literature, and in films, comics and television adaptations. The question, always, will be, how did the imagined exploits of such a remotely historical figure and his totally fictitious knights come to achieve such a command of European narrative, how did such a story retain its power to accommodate so many different sentiments and systems of belief, and why does Arthurian romance continue to exert such fascination?

But throughout, the main emphasis will be not on 'explaining' Arthurian romance or providing a historical or cultural context for it, but on awakening or reawakening the interest that these writings once had and still, once read, command. There will be some deliberate attention to the rehearsing of the stories of the most important works, as a preparation for or a reminder of the experience of reading. There is a great gulf between the act of reading and the act of talking about what we have read – the one linear, temporal, emotionally engaged, subtle in its multiple responses, the other compositional, abstract, dispassionate, atemporal, and capable only of distilling out a few discussable topics from the complex experience of reading. Though it is to the latter that anyone writing a book about Arthurian romance has inevitably to be committed, it is the former, and the enhancement of it, that I want always to have in mind.

I

The Early Arthur

What is the Historical Evidence of a 'Real' Arthur?

A leader, though not one called Arthur, had long been associated with the brave but unavailing defence of the Britons, that is, the Romanized and Christianized Celtic inhabitants of Britain, against the pagan Anglo-Saxon invaders in the late fifth and early sixth centuries. The most authentic historical story is that told by Bede (673–735), monk of Wearmouth and Jarrow, in his Latin *Historia ecclesiastica gentis Anglorum* ('Ecclesiastical History of the English People'), completed in 731, and supported by fairly reliable continental sources and by archaeological finds. It tells of a power vacuum that followed the Roman evacuation of Britain (which was the northernmost province of the empire) in 410, and of resistance to the various continental marauders who were sucked into this vacuum to plunder the rich counties of southern and eastern England and who eventually settled there.

But there was a need for something more dramatic and decisive than this, more intelligible as an explanation of the causes of historical events, whether in the form of a satisfying narrative of general moral sloth punished by military defeat, or in the form of a heroic story of battles bravely won and lost. The retrospect of history needs decisive battles, where a brave warrior can act as the leader of the defeated people so that his final and inevitable defeat in battle can mark the transfer of power to the victors, the *translatio imperii*.

Gildas, a British (that is, Celtic) monk of the mid-sixth century (d. 570), is the earliest witness for the story of a concerted British resistance, under a named leader, against the Anglo-Saxon invaders. His account of events was known to Bede, and appears in his ranting tract *De excidio et conquestu Britanniae* ('Concerning the Destruction and Conquest of Britain'), probably written after he had departed for Brittany. Gildas is not interested, at this early date, in foundation myths of legitimation. For him the Anglo-Saxon conquest is a punishment visited by God upon an erring people – an explanation that was always available to medieval monkish writers to deal with disasters of all kinds, from earthquakes and plagues to a succession of particularly disreputable popes.

The lack of evidence for Arthur's existence in Gildas is startling, given that he is a datable witness, writing near the time when Arthur is supposed to have existed, and about the battles in which he is supposed to have played a prominent part. Gildas does mention a British leader who around the year 500 fought a great battle against the Anglo-Saxons at Mount Badon (Mons Badonicus, probably on Salisbury Plain, where the Saxons were indeed for a time halted), but the name he gives him is not Arthur but Ambrosius Aurelianus, clearly representative of that old Romano-Christian-British civilization whose passing Gildas laments with such gloomy relish. 'A gentleman', he calls him, 'who, perhaps alone of the Romans, had survived the shock of this notable storm: certainly his parents, who had worn the purple, were slain in it. His descendants in our day have become greatly inferior to their grandfather's excellence' (25.3, p. 28).

The absence of early written evidence for Arthur is, as I say, startling, but it does not in itself mean that Arthur did not exist. In the absence of written records of any kind, other than the tainted witness of a writer like Gildas, much will be lost, and some will be lost absolutely, and the two centuries after the departure of the Romans are an exceptionally blank period. An instructive comparison is made by the historian Gerald Hammond in a review of a book on early Mayan history. He writes:

> Only in the 1970s did Mayan history begin to emerge, as the dynasties of Tikal, Palenque and Copan and other great cities of the first millennium A.D. were transformed from simple lists of kings to a chronicle of their martial and marital exploits on thousands of carved stelae, door-lintels and other media. Kings such as Jasaw Chan K'awiil I of Tikal and K'inich Janaab' Pakal I of Palenque left such elaborate and

explicit records that we know more about both of them than we know about King Arthur.[1]

Scholars of King Arthur would give anything for a single one of those thousands of inscriptions, whether on a pillar, a post, a lintel, a stone, or any other kind of durable material. In the absence of such writing, we know next to nothing of King Arthur. The best we have is an ancient slab, still to be found on the banks of the River Camel, near Camelford, in Cornwall, near the supposed site of the legendary 'last battle' at Camlann, where Arthur and Mordred died. It has Ogham script as well as Latin and can be dated to the sixth century. The Latin inscription, so far as it can be made out, reads 'LATINI IACIT FILIUS MA. . . . RI'. Arthurian enthusiasts since the early seventeenth century have hoped that this could refer to Arthur, and a small Arthurian theme-park, opened in 2000 near the site, celebrates 'King Arthur's Stone', as well as much else of Arthurian legend, though it also displays clearly the almost conclusive evidence against any Arthurian association.

But there was an 'Arthur' floating about in Welsh legend. He is first recorded in the *Gododdin*, a commemoration of British heroes who fell at Caetrath (Catterick) about 600 AD, written by Aneirin; a Welsh poet who is presumed to have flourished in the seventh century but whose writings are preserved only in manuscripts from the thirteenth. Aneirin offers superlative praise of the hero Gwawrddur, 'but', he adds, 'he was not Arthur'. That is the first we hear of him: he was already a pre-eminent hero (and his name provided a convenient rhyme). In later Welsh legend, Arthur has the reputation of a warrior of superhuman powers, not particularly virtuous, in fact not virtuous at all, and certainly not a Christian – a winner of giant cauldrons, a killer of monstrous cats, and the stealer of the comb and scissors from between the ears of Twrch Trwyth, the terrible Chief Boar of the Island of Britain. It seems to have been in the *Historia Brittonum*, a collection of historical notes attributed, probably wrongly, to an early ninth-century monk called Nennius, that Arthur first appeared as a great patriotic Christian national leader (*dux bellorum*, 'leader of battles', not king) killed in the triumphant and decisive last charge at Mount Badon (516). His name in Nennius is 'Arthur', which was derived from the well-attested Roman name Artorius, and which had some unprecedented currency among the Celts of Britain in the sixth century. A similar story is alluded to in the *Annales Cambriae*, a collection of historical notes surviving in a Latin manuscript of *c.*1100 but deriving from much earlier Celtic legends, of a battle at Badon in 516 where Arthur carried the cross of Jesus for three days on his shoulder and the British were the victors. There is also here a reference to a battle at Camlann in 539 in which Arthur and Medraut (Mordred) perished. So, from the ninth century, the battle-leader of Mount Badon, now for the first time named as Arthur, became a great hero, around whom began to accrete legends associated with the 'Arthur' of Celtic folklore, who may or may not be the same person (if there ever was one).

There is, it is clear, no simple answer, indeed no answer at all, to the question, 'Was there a real Arthur?' Faced with total frustration in trying to answer a question so simple, it is interesting to wonder if it was necessary to ask it in the first place. The desire to ask it, and the determination to arrive at a positive answer, has always been strong, as is evident in the account of the disinterment of the supposed Arthur's skeletal remains at Glastonbury in 1191 or in Caxton's determination to prove Arthur historical in his Preface to Malory's *Morte D'Arthur* (1485) by offering evidence on the present whereabouts of Lancelot's sword, Gawain's skull and the Round Table. On these occasions there were, it is true, particular reasons for trying to prove that Arthur was a real person: the abbey of Glastonbury was eager to use Arthur to establish its special venerable antiquity and with that its exemption from episcopal visitation, while Caxton was making the usual publisher's claim to have the full, true and authentic story. But even when there are no such practical reasons, the desire for a real Arthur still remains strong, as can be seen from the caravans of TV cameramen and newshounds and assorted well-wishers who have accompanied every supposed archaeological sighting of Arthur, such as that at Cadbury Camp in Somerset in 1966, and who remain on the alert for every Arthurian promotional stunt. It is not very different from the publicity that is given to UFOs.

In a larger sense, the desire to find a historical Arthur can be understood as part of the yearning for 'great men' or heroes, a desire that is powerfully fed by both the idea of the individual and the idea of the subordination of the individual to the will of the leader or to the state. Belief in the power of individuals to change things is writ large in the belief that 'great men', whether dark-age kings or modern presidents and prime ministers, are individuals who can change everything. In this way, attention can be distracted from the painful and intractable realities of social and economic circumstance. The desire to seek a historical Arthur is part of this 'cult of personality', of belief in a great king who changed the course of history. Of course, even in the mythical story, Arthur did not change anything for long, but then he has a further great claim on us as a great man, that is, the attraction of the tragic hero, the survivor of a great civilization fighting a desperate rearguard action against barbarians – even if those barbarians, in the end, are *us*, the English, and even if the process was actually one of prolonged and messy integration rather than a doomed heroic last stand. Many British people stayed and mixed peaceably with the Anglo-Saxons, and many of the battles that were fought were not between nation and nation but between one local faction and another. At the battle of Catterick, around 600, in Welsh poetry a famous heroic battle against the invaders, there were British and Anglo-Saxons fighting on both sides. It is a not uncommon kind of national myth-making: the tangle of events in eighth-century Spain, when the Frankish armies, withdrawing after unsuccessfully encountering the Moorish conquerors of the peninsula, were set upon in the Pyrenees by hostile local groups, had to be simplified for the sake of the narrative of French nationhood into the story of a hero and a villain and of the doomed last stand of the hero Roland at Roncesvalles against the overwhelming might of the infidel.

Winston Churchill, whose *History of the English-speaking Peoples* fits well the idea of history as what 'ought' to have happened, speaks thus of the desire and need for Arthur's historicity:

> It is all true, or ought to be; and more and better besides. And wherever men are fighting against barbarism, tyranny and massacre, for freedom, law and honour, let them remember that the fame of their deeds, even though they themselves be exterminated, may perhaps be celebrated as long as the world rolls round. Let us then declare that King Arthur and his noble knights, guarding the Sacred Flame of Christianity and the theme of a world order, sustained by valour, physical strength, and good horses and armour, slaughtered innumerable hosts of foul barbarians and set decent folk an example for all time.[2]

So Arthur, whether he existed or not, in any form that we might recognize, had to be invented (or found) to fill a vacuum in history and to fulfil a need for a national hero. The nature of his existence as what is supplied is what has made him always so malleably contemporary. He is a vacuum, waiting to be filled with signification, a floating signifier, or, as it is put in the Introduction to the book of essays edited by Shichtmann and Carley – which has much more of this kind of jargon – the legend is 'a set of unstable signs appropriated by differing cultural groups to advance differing ideological agendas'.[3] For this use, Roland was less effective. Though he seems to have been expanded from very modest historical beginnings in order to provide a suitable national Christian hero at the time of the First Crusade in 1099, and though he survived to be transmogrified into romance by the Italian poet Ariosto, his role was too well defined for him to survive in the way Arthur has.

At a deeper level than the cult of the hero, there is also the desire for the narrative of historical inevitability, in which the 'causes' of history will become transparent, and the death of the hero will mark the transfer of power. So, as with Arthur, the American myth of 'manifest destiny' found inevitability and legitimation for the American spread westward in stories of brave and temporarily successful but ultimately doomed defensive actions led by famous Indian warriors. Sitting Bull and Geronimo are the modern equivalents of Arthur in this account: it is interesting that Sitting Bull is also associated with legends of a second coming, when buffaloes will once more roam the prairies.

Beyond this, there is the simple desire for historical certainty. Renaissance scholars like Milton, having first been enchanted by the Arthurian legends, found disenchantment in scornful rejection of their claims to veracity. This attitude has come to be regarded as scientific and objective, but proving that Arthur did not exist is just as impossible as proving that he did. On this matter, like others, it is good to think of the desire for certainty as the pursuit of an illusion.

Geoffrey of Monmouth

By the early twelfth century Arthur already had a long career, as we have seen, in Celtic legend, most of it oral, and surviving in written form only in later copies from no earlier than the thirteenth century. He appears frequently in the collection of Welsh prose tales known as the *Mabinogion*, and presumed to date from the late eleventh and twelfth centuries. He is often associated with other warriors who have a permanent place in the later Arthurian tradition, and particularly with Cei (Kay) and Bedwyr (Bedivere). He first appears as the king of a well-known court in a tale from this collection called *Culhwch and Olwen*, perhaps to be dated as early as 1100. That his fame had spread beyond Celtic-speaking lands is evident from the remarkable survival in Italy of a semi-circular sculpted stone frieze over the north door-way of Modena cathedral. It shows 'Artus de Bretania' and others fighting, named in carved labels, and is usually dated not later than about 1120.[4] But even allowing for this enigmatic fragment of evidence, and for the persistence of Arthur in Celtic legend, it seems that Arthur would probably have gone the way of Cuchulainn and other Celtic heroes, into a more narrowly circumscribed cultural history, if it had not been for Geoffrey of Monmouth (d. 1154), whose Latin prose *Historia regum Britanniae* ('History of the Kings of Britain'), written between 1130 and 1136, is one of the most influential books ever written. The *Historia* is not itself a romance – in fact it masquer-ades as a meticulously exact account of British history, with details of the reigns of kings who never existed and of the numbers killed in battles that never took place – but it was the pseudo-historical basis on which the whole story of Arthur was erected.

Geoffrey studied and taught at Oxford, and spent much of his life there as a professional cleric, though he held ecclesiastical offices elsewhere, such as that of archdeacon of Llandaff. He had close associations with the aristocracy, especially Robert, earl of Gloucester (d. 1147), one of the most powerful men in the kingdom and one of the dedicatees of the *Historia*. Geoffrey was consecrated bishop of St Asaph in 1152 (a week after being ordained priest), but he never visited his see, and died in 1154.

Over two hundred manuscripts of the Latin text of the *Historia* are extant, a quite staggering number, given the probable survival rates of manuscripts of a non-religious text from such an early period, and suggestive of thousands that have perished. It was further dissem-inated in French and English translations. Not only is the *Historia* the primary and direct source for the whole central supposedly historical story of Arthur, it is also the only source for stories such as those of King Lear and Cymbeline (both of them the subject of plays by Shakespeare), and the lesser-known King Lud, who gave his name to

London, and King Bladud, who met his death over London in an early attempt to fly. Geoffrey begins with Brutus, an otherwise unknown great-grandson of Aeneas, who gathered the remnants of the Trojan race after the destruction of Troy and sailed to the distant isle of Albion, which he renamed Britain, after himself. There he founded the city of Troynovant, or New Troy (a rationalization of Trinovantes, which Geoffrey had come across as the name of a historical British tribe that lived east and north of London in pre-Roman times), later called London, after King Lud, of course. Geoffrey carries the history of Britain down to the death of Cadwallader (d. 689), an actual historical person and the last 'British', that is, Welsh, king with serious claims to dominion in England. In between, he alternates fairly rapid series of kings with more developed narratives of Leir, of Belinus and Brennius and their conquest of Gaul and Rome, of the Roman invasions of Britain, and of Uther Pendragon and Arthur.

Geoffrey used Gildas, Bede and Nennius, and took much from traditional Welsh legend, of which he had an extensive knowledge, and from Breton legend. Some of it would have been oral, but some too would have been written: the fact that the Welsh material he used is known to us now only in copies made after his death does not mean that he did not use earlier written sources which have since disappeared. But he also unquestionably invented a great deal too, especially in the early part of his narrative, his purpose being to supply England with the national history, the myth of national emergence, that it lacked. The Romans traced their ancestry to the Trojan hero Aeneas, in the story told by Virgil in the *Aeneid*, and other peoples claimed Trojan heroes as their eponymous ancestors, the Lombards, for instance, claiming Langobardus and the Franks Francus. Virgil was the great model for emulation, and because of him the Trojans were generally the heroes of the Trojan war in the medieval view, the Greeks being regarded as a shifty and treacherous race. Geoffrey's purpose was to claim descent for Britain from Troy, and also to create a great national hero, in whom the nation would be symbolized, in the person of Arthur. Geoffrey alleges that he derived the new parts of his work, the stories so far untold, from 'a certain very ancient book, written in the British language' (*britannici sermonis librum vetustissimum*), owned by his friend Walter, the well-attested archdeacon of Oxford, and originating in Brittany (which would conveniently explain why no one in England had seen it before). The book had unfortunately disappeared since he had used it. He warns rival historians that they have no chance of competing with him on early British history. He has scooped the pool. Contemporary historians of a more sober cast of mind, such as William Newburgh, were scornful of his 'History', but Geoffrey was by now working, so to speak, in a different genre.

It is an amazing feat of invention. Probably half of Geoffrey's ninety-nine kings between Brutus and Cadwallader are totally made up, though one could not tell this from the plausible-sounding names he invents for them: nothing sounds more improbable than Rud Hud Hudibras, Dunvallo Molmutius or Gurguit Barbtruc, but these are all names Geoffrey could have found in old Welsh genealogies. Geoffrey's inventions are dressed up as perfectly sober matter-of-fact history, with synchronized dating references to Old Testament history, and a particular fondness for explaining the derivation of place-names. His battle-descriptions are detailed and circumstantial, full of military tactics and replete with statistics of the size of the armies and the numbers killed. Sometimes the numbers don't quite add up, which of course suggests that they are drawn from much older sources that may be confused about such things – for clearly, someone who was making them up would get them right.

These inventions force us to ask an odd question: Did Geoffrey know the difference between what was believed to be historically true and what he knew he had made up? There are two possible answers, or rather two more questions. One is, Are narrative historians always sure they know the difference between the two? The second, In what ways does it matter? There was a Carolingian hagiographer or writer of saints' lives of the eighth century who acknowledged that he had no information on certain of the saints whose lives he had written. In such cases, he says, he had made up lives for them of an appropriate kind, knowing that God would guide his pen just as he had guided their lives.[5] In other words, they are portrayed as living the edifying lives they must have lived, and those lives are in that sense more true and, even, more real than the lives they might have lived in actuality, if that actuality were known about, or if indeed they had actually existed. To deduce, from this, that the Middle Ages had no understanding of the difference between fact and fiction is to imply that the difference modern people wish to make is the best or only one there is. The 'very ancient book in the British language' most probably never existed, but it is unlikely that Geoffrey's purpose was to practise upon the gullibility of his audience and patrons, or to share a joke with them about the gullibility of others, or to induce a whimsical and amused complicity such as later authors might indulge when they constructed elaborate framing narratives of pseudo-authentication, like Umberto Eco in *The Name of the Rose*. What Geoffrey was chiefly doing was to secure authority and credit for his version of the history that needed to be written by claiming for it a lost and venerable antiquity. He was supplying the written record of the British history that had been lost.

It may also seem odd, in a way, that Geoffrey should write in praise of the British and be so severe upon the Anglo-Saxons, when he came of and was writing for an Anglo-Norman aristocracy whose supreme recent achievement had been in conquering those very same Anglo-Saxons and colonizing their country. Representing them as untitled holders of the land would reflect poorly on their conquerors. What we mean by 'English' or 'British' is a hard question here, when a Celtic people, most numerous in his day only in Wales, Scotland and Ireland, are celebrated at the expense of the Anglo-Saxon people (who constitute most of the population of England) by victorious Norman people from France who are descended from the Viking invaders of Normandy. What we can point to are the close links between the Anglo-Normans and the Welsh, as indeed those links are present in Geoffrey's own name, which associates him with both; and how the whole story works as a legitimation of serial invasion and conquest from Brutus on, and also, especially in the emphasis on Arthur's continental conquests, as a legitimation of Angevin imperial ambitions. But there are many other topical allusions and reworkings of themes relevant to the contemporary preoccupations of the Anglo-Norman aristocracy: for instance, the very favourable view of Brittany throughout, as Arthur's closest ally, is relevant to Henry I's attempts to woo the Duchy of Brittany into an alliance. In this way, as often, Arthurian legend provided a narrative that would, with appropriate modifications, make the views of a particular political group look like the way things had always been and had to be.

Geoffrey gives particular prominence to Arthur, who occupies about a quarter of the whole work. His *Historia* is in prose, but announces its epic ambition by being divided into the classic twelve books, of which Books 9, 10 and part of 11 deal with Arthur. Before that, Merlin plays a major part. Book 7 contains the 'Prophecies of Merlin', a series of riddling pseudo-prophecies that identify the actors of future history as symbolic animals and lend themselves therefore to fulfilment in a very large number of ways. The Prophecies were written prior to the *Historia* and then incorporated in it, but they were soon detached and in circulation separately. There were many wild and whirling imitations, and this genre of 'political prophecy' is mocked by the Fool in *King Lear* (III.ii). Merlin is also the principal character in Book 8, which ends with the tricking of Ygerna and the engineering of Arthur's conception. Book 9 deals with Arthur's accession, his battles against the Saxons, his marriage to Guenevere, the establishment of his court, his campaigns in Norway and Gaul (against the French king Frollo, whom Arthur kills in single combat before the opposing armies with a single blow which splits Frollo's head into two halves), the holding of his first plenary court at Caerleon (City of the Legions, a Roman city in south Wales to which Geoffrey transferred Arthur's main castle from its traditional Celtic location in Cornwall), and the arrival of the Roman embassy to demand tribute. Book 10 begins with Arthur's dream of the bear and the dragon, and goes on to narrate the arrival at Barfleur, the fight against the giant of Mont-Saint-Michel, Gawain's embassy to Rome, the ambush of pursuing Romans after his hurried departure, the ambush of the British taking prisoners to Paris, and the battle of Saussy (which occupies almost half the book). Book 11 tells of Mordred's treachery and Arthur's three battles against him, ending with the battle of Camblan, which Geoffrey dates to 542 AD, and the carrying away of Arthur, mortally wounded, to the Isle of Avalon. The crown passes to his cousin Constantine, and Book 12 tells of his successors, now in effect kings of Wales only, until Cadwallader finally abandons Britain to the Saxons.

Most of the familiar story of King Arthur, it will be seen, is already here, though there is as yet no Round Table, and his followers are either relatives, like Gawain and Mordred, or household servants, like his seneschal Kay and his cup-bearer Bedivere, or else tributary kings and dukes, like Cador, and not feudal knights. But there are the beginnings of a court such as will provide in the future a setting for romantic adventures and entanglements. Arthur's first crown-wearing at Caerleon, to which all the leaders of the British come to pay homage, is elaborately described, and includes the first-ever reference to a battle-game or tournament fought for fun, where the ladies wore the colours of their menfolk and 'aroused them to passionate excitement by their flirtatious behaviour' (ix.14, p. 230). We seem to be suddenly in the high Middle Ages here, though we come back to earth with the rest of the day's sports, which include playing dice and heaving heavy stones and rocks around.

Elsewhere, though, Geoffrey gives little attention to women as objects of romantic attachment. Cador's contribution to the discussion of the demands of the Roman ambassadors is to welcome the opportunity of some serious fighting since the long spell of peace has left men unused to their weapons, 'playing at dice, and burning up their strength with women' (ix.15, p. 232). Earlier, the story of Uther's passion for Ygerne has none of the trappings of the ideal medieval code of love. Uther simply burns with passion and has to find a way of satisfying it: it is his destiny. Nor is there any investigation of Ygerne's feelings on the matter, no debate about whether she really thought it was her husband in bed with her such as we might think inseparable from the notion of identity; she seems to accept what has happened quite peaceably when she finds out, though the fact that her husband Gorlois turns out to have been conveniently killed, just the minute before Uther jumped into bed with her, makes things easier to bear. Geoffrey's rationalizations are interesting here: he recognizes, and has as witness the stories of the birth of both Alexander the Great and Jesus Christ, that the greatest heroes must be born of mysterious conceptions, with supernatural interventions as a form of suprahistorical legitimization, but he stops short of having Arthur born of any but a (just about) legal union or of any but the king.

Geoffrey is equally perfunctory in describing Arthur's marriage to Guenevere. She is introduced simply as 'a woman called Guenevere' (ix.9) and within two sentences he is married to her. Later, Geoffrey's professed reluctance to comment on Guenevere's adulterous liaison with Mordred may be a form of gentlemanly discretion, or a passing claim to veracity (refusal to talk about something suggests to the reader that there is something real to talk about), but it is more likely to be evidence of his lack of interest in the desires and feelings of men and women in their sexual relationships with each other. For him, battles and skirmishes, strategies and slaughters, are the stuff of history, especially when religion can be called in to sanction them: Archbishop Dubricius guarantees salvation to those who die in Arthur's cause, and Arthur himself carries an image of the Blessed Virgin on his shield as he rushes forward with his sword into the thick of battle. 'Every man whom he struck, calling upon God as he did so, he felled at a single blow' (ix.4, p. 217).

Wace, *Roman de Brut*

Geoffrey's *Historia* was written in Latin, which was the *lingua franca* of educated or literate people (the original meaning of Latin *litteratus*, 'literate', was 'literate in Latin'), and therefore principally of clerics, who were the only people who were normally taught Latin. But its impact was such that it was soon translated into French, which was the aristocratic *lingua franca* of western Europe (and remained so in Italy until the time of Dante, in England until the time of Chaucer). A rhymed translation, the *Estorie des Bretons*, no longer extant, was made about 1150 by the Anglo-Norman Geffrei Gaimar. It was soon superseded by another French version, also in octosyllabic couplets, called by its author the *Geste des Bretons* ('The History of the Britons'), but soon renamed by scribes the *Roman de Brut* to fit it to the new fashions. This very free translation, or rather expanded adaptation, was made by Robert Wace, a cleric from Jersey in the Channel Islands who had settled in Caen in Normandy, and presented to Eleanor of Aquitaine, the imperious and flamboyant new queen of Henry II, in 1155. This puts the work immediately at the heart of European courtly culture, for the court of Henry II (reigned 1154–89) and the glamorous divorcée Eleanor was the most exciting in Europe. Henry's power extended over most of France as well as England, and the court and literary language of his kingdom was French.

Wace follows the sequence of events in Geoffrey pretty closely, but he constantly adapts the story to the fashions of a more courtly and chivalric and self-consciously elegant culture. His work takes its place among the many contemporaneizations and romanticizations of earlier stories, especially classical epics, that were being produced in the twelfth century to fit them to the new culture of chivalry and idealized love. There was a *Roman d'Eneas*, a *Roman de Troie*, a *Roman de Thebes*, even a *Roman d'Edippus*, and characteristic of all of them was to stress the elegance of court manners, costume and decoration, and the importance of affairs of the heart. Achilles' relationship with Polyxena takes on a much greater prominence at the siege of Troy, and the whole love-affair of Troilus and Cressida is woven into the story out of nothing. Virgil's story of the love of Aeneas and Lavinia, in the *Roman d'Eneas*, is elevated so as to give it more attention, and a romantic episode is interpolated even into the story of Thebes, though fortunately there is no attempt to romanticize the relationship of Oedipus and Jocasta.

The tone of Wace's treatment is well illustrated in his account of Uther's passion for Igerne. Wace turns Geoffrey's abrupt and rather clinical account of Uther's infatuation into a fashionable public flirtation, with laughs and glances, and with Igerne joining in quite knowingly.

> He glanced aside at the lady, and smiled if she met his eye. All that he dared of love he showed. He saluted her by his privy page, and bestowed upon her a gift. He jested gaily with the lady, looking smilingly upon her, and made a great semblance of friendship. Igerne was modest and discreet. She neither granted Uther's hope, nor denied.
> (p. 36)

Also the signs of love are more elaborately described in Uther according to the codes of behaviour that were beginning to be celebrated as part of the cult of ideal love. No man could really count himself in love unless he thought continually about his beloved, lost his appetite, couldn't sleep, and grew thin and pale, and Uther duly suffers a beginner's version of these symptoms (where in Geoffrey it is simply said that he will have a physical breakdown if he fails to get hold of Ygerne): 'Whether he ate or drank, spoke or was silent, she was ever in his thought'. A curious book, the *De arte honeste amandi* ('The Art of Honest Loving'), written for Eleanor of Aquitaine's daughter (by her first marriage), Marie de Champagne (1145–98), by her chaplain, Andreas Capellanus, gives a seemingly serious list of all the rules of the lovers' behaviour in the service of his lady, as well as model dialogues for the purposes of seduction. It has been sometimes taken seriously, as if it really did provide rules of conduct for real life, or else it has been treated as a covert moralizing attack on fashionably loose sexual morals, but the likeliest explanation seems to be that it is a rather sophisticated and *risqué* send-up of some of the excesses of an erotically charged court atmosphere. The existence of such a parody would argue for a thriving culture of amorous sentiment.

Wace is comparatively restrained in his romanticization of the story of Arthur, perhaps necessarily so because of the nature of the story. Guenevere is declared to be surpassingly beautiful, and Arthur to have set his love wonderfully upon her, which is more than there is in Geoffrey, but the account of their marriage is swiftly brought to an end with the reminder that they had no child together (which Geoffrey forebore to mention). Elsewhere, there is a generally greater emphasis on human feelings and affections than in Geoffrey, and this may be part of the courtly cultivation in the twelfth century of a more refined sensibility, of which the growing interest in romantic love was part. The return of Arthur's lords from the battles against Frollo and the French is described as bringing joy to their ladies, and the love of knights for their ladies and their desire to show well in their sight are prominent in the greatly expanded description of the courtly festivities at Arthur's crown-wearing. But there is no elaboration of love-sentiment such as we shall see in later romance.

Wace's treatment of Geoffrey's story shows also some tentative first moves towards the portrayal of Arthur, though he remains essentially a martial figure. as a chivalric hero. He speaks of him at his cor-o: atic n as a prince of courtesy and 'one of Love's lovers' (p. 43), a conventional enough phrase but one that would have been unthink-able tor Geoffrey. As Arthur prepares for battle near Bath, there is a more fashionably detailed account of his armour and accoutrements than in Geoffrey, and he even has a horse, a proud destrier (p. 48). He does not appear to use it in the ensuing battle, which is fought on foot, Roman style, as in Geoffrey. Wace has spontaneously equipped Arthur with what no hero of chivalric romance (no *chevalier*) can be without. He also suppresses the archbishop Dubricius's exhortation to the troops before the same battle, in which he promises salvation to those who die in this just war for their country, and instead Arthur is given a speech of proud revenge. Arthur is becoming slightly less of a national religious leader and warrior and slightly more of a Europeanized chivalric hero.

Layamon's *Brut*

A hundred years or so after Geoffrey had launched Arthur on his international career, Wace's version of the *Brut*, as it was coming to be called, was taken up by an obscure country priest of Arley Kings, on the River Severn near Worcester, and put into English verse. The *Brut* of Layamon[6] is a complete version of Wace which expands the Arthurian section with great patriotic vigour and enthusiasm and has many claims to be the first or even the only true English national epic.

> Hit com him on mode & on his mern thonke
> Thet he wolde of Engle tha æthelen tellen.
>
> (lines 6–7)

[It came into his mind and into his high purpose that he would tell of the noble deeds of the English.]

The 'English', as we know them, were strictly speaking the villains of the piece and not the heroes, but in charting all the patterns of conquest and movements of allegiance it is his passionate attachment to the 'land of Britain' that gives Layamon's work its national epic temper.

Layamon does not misunderstand or always neglect Wace's courtly interventions in Geoffrey, but he works against Wace in creating a heroic and martial rather than a courtly and chivalric atmosphere, and in portraying Arthur as a fierce warrior-king. Layamon is inspired by strong national and patriotic feelings which found little opportunity for expression while he was labouring after Wace in the early part of the history, king by confected king, but Arthur provides a focus for all his patriotic and imaginative energies and all his love of heroic battle-poetry. It is on these occasions that Layamon, who writes an idiosyncratic mixture of traditional unrhymed alliterative poetry derived from Anglo-Saxon and rhyming or assonantal couplets derived from Wace, seems closest to the Germanic heroic spirit of poems like the *Fight at Finnesburh* and the *Battle of Maldon*.

The general character of Layamon's *Brut* can be illustrated from some comparisons with Wace. Wace's first introduction of Arthur in person is cool, measured, generalized and abstract, proposing to tell without exaggeration of one who surmounted all in courtesy and nobility, virtue and liberality. Layamon excises all comment on love and courtesy and concentrates on particular detail to build up a portrait of extravagant heroism and kingliness, steeped in religious awe.

In the battles with the Saxons, Layamon writes with brilliant panache, bringing his poem to a climax as he comes to the treacherous raid by the Saxons on the south-west after they have made a truce with Arthur. The account in Wace is generalized and well articulated, with the sequence and geography of events in clear perspective; Layamon is full of graphic, violent, often inessential detail, poured out pell-mell as if the verse can hardly contain the fury and indignation and bitter foreshadowing irony concerning the fate of the perfidious Saxons. The battle of Bath brings this sequence to a climax: Wace prepares for it with a careful description of Arthur's advance and an elaborate and solemn speech of exhortation, before describing the battle quite briefly (more briefly than Geoffrey, who as usual gives a precise and circumstantial account of battlefield and general strategy). These careful preparations are almost swept aside in the onrush of Layamon's martial fervour (which has the love of violence characteristic of those who have occupations that keep them well away from any actual fighting), with vigorous scenes of individual combat and mêlée punctuated with vows of vengeance, boastings, denunciation, execration, scorn and triumph, and ending with Arthur's sarcastic tauntings over the defeated Saxons as they flee and are drowned in the River Avon (10638–42):

> Yurstendæi wes Baldulf cnihten alre baldest;
> nu he stant on hulle and Avene bihaldeth;
> hu ligeth i than stræme stelene fisces,
> mid sweorde bigeorede. Heore sund is awemmed;
> heore scalen wleoteth swulc gold-faȝe sceldes.

[Yesterday Baldulf was the boldest of knights; now he stands on a hill and looks upon the Avon, how there lie in the stream steel fishes, equipped with swords. Their swimming-power is impaired! Their scales gleam like gilded shields.]

Throughout Wace is calm, practical, rational, with an eye for the realities of war and strategy; Layamon is aggressive, violent, heroic, ceremonial and ritualistic.

Arthur's battles against the Saxons illustrate how Layamon makes a drama out of what in Geoffrey and Wace was more like a chronicle: the difference is like that between the Bayeux tapestry, with each episode given the same sort of attention, and a huge epic battle-scene.

There is a much stronger sense of emotional identification with Arthur and the British, shown in Arthur's speech to his troops before the battle of Lincoln (10287–98) – a noble exhortation to them to destroy those who have brought calamity upon Britain, and to avenge our kinsmen and their realm, 'ure cun and heore riche' (10297). The attachment to the British cause is strong enough to permit even some criticism of Arthur, as an individual with a capacity for human error, in the suggestion that he was headstrong and rash in allowing a truce when he did (10428): 'Her wes Arthur the king athelan bidæled' ('. . . lacking in sound judgement'). Elsewhere, in the same spirit of emotional identification, there is exaggeration of enemy atrocities, insulting ironies at their expense, and ominous foreshadowing of the fate that awaits them. The 'epic similes' that are so prominent a feature of Layamon's style in this section are strongly emotive in spirit: Arthur is compared to a savage wolf, a raging wild boar, his foes to fleeing cranes or wretched foxes dug out of their holes by hunters.

Another distinctive feature of Layamon's treatment of Arthur is his serious-minded attention to the establishment of an ordered kingdom under the rule of law. After the campaigns against the Saxons are over, Arthur holds the kingdom for many years in peace, but eventually disagreements about precedence among his diverse followers break out in open brawling at a feast and many are killed. Arthur deals with the problem by first executing those responsible for starting the fight, and having the noses of their womenfolk cut off so that no one will want to marry them and the tribe will die out. Having thus established law and order in his own unique way, he has the Round Table installed, at which there can be no disputes about precedent. The Round Table was very briefly mentioned by Wace, but here it is made much of, with an explanatory story. It is, contrary to most modern portrayals, a hollow rather than a solid disc, with people sitting inside facing those on the outside (11436). It is said to travel everywhere with Arthur, but this, since it is big enough to seat 1600, would have presented problems. Layamon is quite careful to distance himself from the story at such points. 'This was that table', he says, 'of which Britons boast, telling fables of many kinds about Arthur' (11454–5), and warns about the dangers of speaking from personal prejudice before himself going on to state as plain fact that there was never any king like Arthur. The air of painfully honest truth-telling makes what he says appear to be no more than the truth. He introduces the same note of caution in speaking of the belief of the Britons that Arthur dwells still in Avalon and will return one day to help the people of England. It was, he says, with all the air of someone bringing weighty evidence to bear, one of Merlin's prophecies, and 'his sayings were true' (14296). In this, and in every other way, Layamon shows his care for his reputation as a historian, and not a romancer.

2

The Romancing of the Arthurian Story: Chrétien de Troyes

There will be a continuing life for King Arthur as a military commander and national hero in the fourteenth-century alliterative poem of the *Morte Arthure* and in Malory, but the major new development after Geoffrey of Monmouth is the 'romancing' of the Arthurian story that began to be hinted at in Wace.

The transition from national epic to courtly romance is the result of the transplantation of Arthur from England to France. When a story is removed from its nation or people and transplanted into a different culture, it tends to lose its heroic national temper and be made the vehicle for more generally fashionable social concerns. In France, which is where courtly romance grew up, those concerns had to do with love and chivalry, and the society for which it began to cater is one characterized by the emergence of a more leisured aristocracy, with more of a place ostensibly given to women, ideals and codes of ideal behaviour, all of them comprised in the term 'chivalry'. In the English tradition from which he was transplanted, King Arthur himself had a very limited romantic interest: he has no interesting love-affairs either before or after his early marriage. It seems impossible to imagine any being invented for him. So in Arthurian romance he is relegated to the role of, at best, a great king who stays at home while his knights go off on romantic adventures and report back to him, or, at worst, an ineffectual cuckold. Nothing is said of his campaigns against the Saxons and the Romans. Arthurian romance has Arthur's court as its background or point of reference, but it is not about Arthur.

The Chivalric Love-Romance

Romance is the literature of chivalry and exists to reflect, celebrate and confirm the chivalric values by which its primary consumers, the noble or knightly class, live or purport to live. It does not record their way of life so much as how they would like to think of themselves and be thought of as living, without the frustrations and expediencies of real life. Romance purges life of impurities and presents chivalry in heightened and idealized form. Northern France in the late twelfth century – the society of Eleanor of Aquitaine and Marie de Champagne and the clerk-poet Chrétien de Troyes, leisured, wealthy, sophisticated, woman-orientated, culturally ambitious – is the most exciting venue for the new romance, but the great cities of the late Hohenstaufen Empire are not far behind.

The nature of romance may be seen clearly from a comparison with epic, which is the literature of the more warlike and male-centred society that dominated in western Europe until the twelfth century. Heroic stories such as that of King Arthur are the celebration of the values of this society, most of which have to do with fighting. The setting is historical or quasi-historical; the events and persons are assumed to be real as well as important. The central realities of heroic literature are not love or honour but loyalty to one's kin or leader, revenge, and the imperative necessity of asserting self (especially self as embodying a nation or people) through acts of power. Women are important in epic because of their essential role in the action, as part of the urging towards power, possession and revenge which are the source of action, not as ideals or as objects of adoration. Men fight for them because if they don't the women will be killed, raped or otherwise forced into subjection, not because they will be upset.

Romance, by contrast, deals in adventure, not survival. The hero is not desperately defending his homeland but chooses to go out from a secure bastion of wealth and privilege (such as the Arthurian court) to seek adventures in which the values of chivalry and service to ladies (not only being in love but 'being a lover', a social grace as much as a private emotion) will be submitted to test and proved. 'The series of adventures', as Auerbach puts it, 'is thus raised to the status of a fixed and graduated test of election; it becomes the basis of a doctrine of personal perfection'.[1] Courage is still important, but now in the service of an ideal code of values, not as a necessity for survival: in theory that code could require cowardice of the hero (as in Chrétien's *Lancelot*). The action is no longer 'real' or historical; there are elements of the marvellous; geography is vague; time is unreal. The knight is not impelled by dynastic or territorial ambitions, but chooses to go out on adventures because that is how he proves the values by which he lives – proves his reality, his identity, in fact. Feats of arms, arbitrary in themselves, are the means to self-realization. Action has no exterior real motivation: there is no reason, in Chrétien's *Yvain*, for Laudine's husband to defend the spring, nor for Arthur to ravage the country if it is left undefended. Above all, the hero now thinks and feels as well as acts; there is an inner consciousness to be explored. He is in love.

The new concentration on love in Arthurian romance has to do with new audiences and newly civilized courts; it has also to do with a revolution in the attitude to and representation of sensibility that began in the twelfth century and quickly gathered power – the growth of the idea that human emotion is not a disease of the will nor an enemy of the reason but an attribute to be valued for its potential to inspire nobility of behaviour. It was not a change of sensibility or a reformation of the human heart so much as a change in the cultural opportunities for the representation of sensibility. In secular courtly culture, this change contributed importantly to the new idea that sexual love was a high form of service. The term 'courtly love' is often applied to this new form of love-service, and though it would not do to simplify into a single universal medieval phenomenon a whole range of social and cultural practices which varied by region, by period, by class, by cultural inheritance and in the work of individual writers, it is nevertheless true that the attachment of an exquisite refinement of ideal sentiment to the love of man and woman is the distinctive characteristic feature of medieval chivalric romance. The new element, and what distinguishes *fine amour* ('fine loving') most clearly from other forms of human sexual love, is the belief in the value of sexual love as an intrinsically ennobling experience, in which the lover's aim is not the satisfaction of desire but progress and growth in virtue, merit and worth. It is the male lover that is referred to, of course, since femininity (of which the female person is a cipher) is already constituted as the essence of these qualities.

In truth, though, the character of the new Arthurian love-romance needs little explanation to modern readers, for it has had eight centuries of life to make it familiar. Wherever pre-marital or non-marital sexual love between men and women is represented in fiction, drama, opera or film as the most important experience of life, wherever the love of a man for a woman *paramours* ('in the way of sexual love') is represented as the service of the highest ideal of existence ('love has made me a better man') – that is to say, in the whole tradition cf romantic and Romantic poetry and drama and in the whole tradition of the novel of courtship (the dominant mode of the nineteenth-century novel) and its successors in the modern romantic novelette – the inheritance of medieval courtly romance is present. Until recent years, it was the dominant theme and troping device of western secular narrative, lyric and drama. It seemed to be 'the way things were', and the constructedness of this code of love, and particularly the manner in which it privileged the male experience of sexual desire at the same time as it figured him as the servant of the female, has only been fully analysed in recent years, primarily in the work of feminist critics.

The appeal of these romances, as exciting and enigmatic stories of passion and idealism that engage our interest and feelings, is obvious, but they claim our attention also in embodying the social and political attitudes, needs and fears of their authors, patrons and audiences and the class to which they belonged. This is what we shall find throughout the history of Arthurian romance, and Stephen Knight is surely right, in *Arthurian Literature and Society*, in aiming to show how the reshapings over a thousand years of the Arthurian legend are politically and historically embedded in the society of their authors. As he says,

> The texts are potent ideological documents through which both the fears and hopes of the dominant class are realized . . . they reveal under close study just what the ruling forces in each period were worried about and how their cultural support-system was able to deflect and partly to console those worries.[2]

Knight refers to a study of early French Arthurian romance by the French economic historian Georges Duby, in which Duby shows how romance served to resolve tensions between the upper and lower ranks of household knights, and between barons and king, by offering to unite all in a common idealism (the Round Table is an example).³ They were a kind of propaganda for the established order. They also offered an idealized account of the way in which the potentially restless group of young landless knights, the *juventes*, excluded from the patrimonial inheritance and yet clearly of gentle birth, could win a fortune by force of arms and marry a rich heiress. That this was no mere escapist fantasy is well demonstrated in the career of an adventurer-knight like William Marshall, in the early thirteenth century, though the account of his life in the romance of *Guillaume le Maréchal* is inevitably somewhat fanciful.

It is sensible to recognize that the 'idealism' of Arthurian romance has its roots in the needs of a particular class and in the conflicts and stresses within that class. In another way, too, French romances serve the purposes of a newly powerful and centralized French monarchy. The glamorizing of a royal court at which barons would attend for long periods, and so be prevented from building up a power-base in their own provincial lands, was very much in the interests of the monarchy (the same technique of control was later used by the Japanese shoguns). One of the striking things about Anglo-Norman romance, that is, the romances written in England in the thirteenth century for the French-speaking English aristocracy, is the almost complete absence of Arthurian themes. The explanation that has been offered is that Arthurian romance, with its image of a strongly centralized monarchy and of Arthur not as *primus inter pares* ('first among equals') but as a divinely endorsed super-king, did not appeal too much to the powerful Anglo-Norman barons.⁴ They much preferred to view the king as one of them, raised to high eminence by their assent, and always liable to be called to account, as King John was in 1215. So, by contrast, the corpus of Anglo-Norman romance includes many 'ancestral romances' that create a noble and ancient pedigree for the existing Anglo-Norman families by recounting the noble exploits of a putative founder. In this way a comparatively newly planted aristocracy could assure itself of roots in the country in which they were settled.

Social and economic and political circumstances are important to the understanding of medieval Arthurian romances, but they do not explain everything. The romances have a life as literature which goes far beyond these origins. We should never underestimate the

charismatic power of stories as stories. Stories are precious inherit-
ances; they have powers and meanings that cannot readily be subdued to the imperatives of socio-economic reality. They have a shape
which is intrinsically satisfying and they partake of the numinous
power of myth. The story of Arthur himself, with its trajectory of rise,
flourishing and decline, has such a shape. On a more practical level,
one can see the attraction of the Arthurian legend as an infinitely
expandable narrative portmanteau. Arthur's court was an extremely
convenient all-purpose location for stories of all kinds, and there
were, surely, enough knights of the Round Table to provide pro-
agonists for almost any story of adventure. The gravitational pull of
hur's court is exemplified in extreme form in a very early French
perhaps earlier even than Chrétien's *Erec*, the *lai* of *Lanval* by
'e France, who was writing in England about 1160–80. It is a
he supernatural, like most of Marie's *lais*, and located in an
arrative realm far to the west of Logres, but Lanval is
knight of Arthur's court, and the king plays a part in
't a weak and indecisive one. He has a queen who
attempted rape when he rejects her advances (an
biblical story of Joseph and Potiphar's wife), but
is unrecognizable as Guenevere.

tien de Troyes

ated by the courtly Provençal poets
s influenced by the sophisticated
hut it was in the late twelfth-
rts in which powerful ladies
hampagne were creating a
display, that these high
sion, above all in th
reatest of the Frec
e shape and
who ir
lity,

eir

of the fine or non-existent line between seriousness and play, as he develops subtle points of love-sentiment, strains the logic of amorous argumentation, and tests the conventionally gendered expectations of behaviour. His poems delight in problems of conduct, especially the problem for the knight-lover of reconciling his chivalric obligations with the imperative of Love, or of mediating between two opposed obligations of honour. In *Lancelot*, for instance, the hero has to debate in his mind between Generosity and Compassion: should he grant the defeated knight mercy, as he must, or kill him as the maiden to whom he has made his promise requests, as he must? His admirable answer to this impossible question is that he will fight him again, this time at a disadvantage, without moving from the spot where he stands (Lancelot, of course, can afford this kind of solution to such a prob-lem, since he always wins). It is a solution to the problem that would have stirred a ripple of applause among the listening audience, and the excitement of these early readings can only be guessed at, with the audience put to many fine debates of 'love-morality' in which women could score as many points as men.

Chrétien's four love-romances – in probable order of composit[ion] *Erec et Enide*, *Cligés*, *Lancelot* (*Le Chevalier de la Charrette*) and *Yvain* *Chevalier au Lion*), each of about 7000 lines in octosyllabic verse the originals and masterpieces of the form. All have Arthurian se[tting] as has the other surviving poem attributed to him, the unf[inished] *Perceval*, or *Le Conte du Graal*, strictly speaking a Grail-roma[nce] not a love-romance.

Lancelot, ou Le Chevalier de la Charrette

Of the four love-romances, one, *Lancelot*, or 'The Knight [of the Cart] is central to the development of the new form. In it La[ncelot] for the first time as a significant figure, with an entire[ ] Guenevere's lover. In the sophisticated court of Marie [ ] [t]o which the poem was introduced, it was the con[vention] fiction's sake and fun, one presumes) that a[lady could] not really love her husband in the way of [lovers and troubado][ur]s) and therefore she must have an adm[irer or] [lo]ver who asked nothing but to worship [ ] to the background, and Lancelot be[comes] [eve]rything – his loyalty to Arthur, his[ ] as a fighting man – for love of Guenevere. According to Chrétien's brief prologue, he was commanded by Marie de Champagne to write this romance, and it was she who provided him with the matter (*matière*) of the story. Whether she did or not, this was a characteristically medieval way of displacing responsibility for the invention of new and possibly controversial material. The introduction of a fashionably adulterous liaison for Guenevere and the conjuring into existence of Lancelot, presumably the *matière* of which he speaks, were certainly the stuff of animated controversy, and perhaps Chrétien, who was a cleric, and whose other love-romances deal with courtship and marital love, felt a particular need to distance himself from such incendiary material.

In the romance, which recounts the kidnapping of Guenevere by Meleagant and Lancelot's adventures in rescuing and avenging her, Lancelot is put through a series of tests in order to show the omnipotence of love, the most extreme being that on occasion he must violate knighthood for Guenevere's sake and at her command. In the episode that gives the romance its subtitle, his horse falls dead from over-riding and he is obliged to ride in a punishment or pillory-cart (one used for criminals) if he is to remain in hot pursuit of the queen and her abductors. He falls into internal debate with himself, such as Chrétien often introduces, before he decides to dishonour himself in this way –

> Reason, who does not follow Love's command, told him to beware of getting in, and admonished and counselled him not to do anything for which he might incur disgrace or reproach. Reason, who dared tell him this, spoke from the lips, not from the heart; but Love, who held sway within his heart, urged and commanded him to climb into the cart at once. Because Love ordered and wished it, he jumped in; since Love ruled his action, the disgrace did not matter. (p. 212)

Later (much later) Guenevere causes him much grief by seeming to reproach him (though she claims afterwards it was only in jest) for ever having thought of delaying for even two steps. On another occasion, in order to determine that the unknown knight who bears down all-comers is really her lover, she sends command that he is to 'do his worst' in the tournament, knowing that only Lancelot would be obedient to his lady to the point of stooping to such shame and dishonour. On another occasion, she is encouraged to give him strength in his battle against Meleagant by appearing in person among the onlookers; she does so, but unfortunately she takes up her station immediately behind where he is fighting. When his attention is drawn to her he cannot take his eyes off her and he must fight his opponent with backhand blows, largely unsuccessfully, until he manages to manoeuvre so that his opponent has his back to Guenevere. Lancelot can fall into such profound reverie at the thought of his beloved that he becomes quite unaware of his surroundings:

> His thoughts were so deep that he forgot who he was; he was uncertain whether or not he truly existed; he was unable to recall his own name, he did not know if he were armed or not, nor where he was going nor whence he came. He remembered nothing at all save one creature, for whom he forgot all others. (p. 216)

Such trance-like meditation has a near-religious quality, and Lancelot's devotion is not infrequently spoken of in religious terms. The crossing of the sword-bridge to the castle where Guenevere is held (the most favoured episode for illustration in illuminated manuscripts of the poem) lacerates his bare hands and feet (he has taken off his gauntlets and shoes to get a better grip), but the pain to him is a kind of martyrdom:

> He crossed in great pain and distress, wounding his hands, knees, and feet. But Love, who guided him, comforted him and healed him at once and turned his suffering to pleasure. (p. 246)

When he finds a comb of Guenevere's with strands of her hair in it, he rhapsodizes over it and reverences it as if it were the relic of a saint.

> He placed the hair on his breast near his heart, between his shirt and his skin. He would not have traded it for a cart loaded with emeralds or carbuncles; nor did he fear that ulcers or any other disease could afflict him; he had no use for magic potions mixed with pearls, nor for drugs against pleurisy, nor for theriaca, nor even for prayers to St Martin and St James.

At moments like this one recognizes both the demonstration and the ironic mockery of the extravagances of this all-consuming passion, and is reminded that medieval audiences loved the rhetoric of casuistry, wit and ingenuity, even when the targets were only exaggerated versions of cherished ideals. One can see, too, how Chrétien might have resorted to irony in order to deal with a certain wistful embarrassment that he might have felt, as a cleric, in glorifying adultery, even at a lady's command.

It is easy to make the romance of Lancelot sound funny, and maybe to overstate the pervasiveness of its irony. For it is a beautiful and mysterious poem, and one that inaugurates all the characteristic strategies of the high Arthurian romance. Everything is enigmatic and unexplained – or at least not explained in any way that is clear until much later, by which time the explanation has been overtaken by other events. Meaning is always elusively beyond reach; the reader's quest mirrors the knight's. Needlessly rash promises, needlessly hidden identities, inexplicable postponements all contribute to the sense of the unknowableness of all outcomes. Beautiful maidens appear who demand to be slept with, knights ride up who demand to be fought with, tombs are come upon with memorial inscriptions for knights not yet dead. Lancelot himself is not named until halfway through the romance, but is called 'the knight', or 'the Knight of the Cart', or 'the knight about whom I have most to say' (p. 236). Lancelot's two fights against Meleagant are the major events of the story, but they are less important than the deferrals, the prolongations, the digressions, that lead up to the moment when Lancelot and Guenevere finally meet or when Lancelot bursts unexpected like a thunderbolt upon his enemy and imperiously bears him down. The narrative movement is everything, as in romantic music the almost endlessly deferred resolution of a harmonic sequence creates delight in the deferral above all.

Lancelot is exceptional among Chrétien's love-romances. The others all have to do with the progress of true love, with all its pains and delights, towards marriage, and the problems in marriage of reconciling the contrary demands of love and honour. The narratives move according to an intelligible design towards an intelligible if not entirely unambiguous conclusion. There is little of the enigma and mystery and bewildering narrative interlacement of Lancelot, which was to have a stronger influence on later Arthurian romance.

Erec et Enide

Erec et Enide was probably the first of Chrétien's romances. Like most of Chrétien's stories and story-episodes, it is derived from Welsh legend and tells of the happy marriage of Erec and Enide, which is disturbed when Enide is overheard by her husband as she laments that she is to blame for what people are calling his uxoriousness and his neglect of feats of arms. This is not something that Erec feels that she is entitled to worry about – it is a betrayal of his high ideal of her as a woman – and he makes her accompany him, for the sake of their love, on an arduous knight-errant journey where, by warning him again and again that he is in danger from surprise attack, she fails repeatedly to resist the temptation to encroach upon his honour, until one day it turns out right. The romance is about the disturbance of the equilibrium between a man and a woman in marriage (as it was perceived in the twelfth century) and how the balance must be restored by acts that cause suffering to both. The theme is reinforced by the inset narrative of the 'Joy of the Court' towards the end. A lady asks her future husband to promise to grant her any request when they are married. He agrees, and it turns out that he has promised to stay with her in an enclosed and enchanted garden until a knight comes along who can defeat him in battle. He would like to be out of the garden and back to the normal life of a knight, but he cannot honourably do anything but his best and so he always wins. Fortunately, Erec is able to defeat him and restore the marriage to the desired equilibrium. A brief summary of the narrative like this is bound to represent the actions of the participants as moving to some conclusion upon which we are to agree, but with Chrétien it has to be admitted that the rights and wrongs of the matter are often elusive: the women in the audience might think that Erec's behaviour towards his beloved wife was unnecessarily severe or even misguided.

The character of the new Arthurian romance is well illustrated in *Erec*. Such romances are rich in joustings and tournaments, in which the hero will often appear incognito so as to be able to win new honour. The actual events of the tournament are highly stylized and repetitive:

> In the mêlée the tumult grew; great was the shattering of lances. Lances were broken and shields were pierced, hauberks dented and torn apart, saddles were emptied, knights fell, horses sweated and foamed. (pp. 63–4)

Their essence is in the hero's superlative display of prowess, honour and courtesy, and his behaviour is what above all is to be attended to and admired. He must know how to conduct himself in battle, but also in court, with his lady, in giving and receiving gifts, in showing piety, in honouring his lord. Our engagement as readers is not with the hero and other characters as individuals, with motives and desires of their own, but as representative actors in the high drama of chivalry. Lancelot will come to be pre-eminent because of the flawless precision, coolness and magnificence with which he shapes his behaviour to the code according to which this drama is played out. Knights, ladies, kings, queens, vavasours, fathers, wives, maidens, all have their proper behaviour mapped onto the complex grid of courtesy, generosity and decorum. They are praised for exhibiting the qualities appropriate to their station and reprimanded for their lack of them or for *desmesure*. Enide is a true lady:

> She was so noble and honourable, wise and gracious in her speech, well-bred and of pleasant company, that no one ever saw in her folly, meanness, or baseness. She had learned so well the social graces that she excelled in all the qualities that any lady must have. (p. 67)

Arthur's court is the place where all these qualities are manifested in their fullest form. It is the school of excellence, where the new code of civilized behaviour has been perfected. It is a code which excludes 'folly, meanness, and baseness' and places many further restraints upon youthful appetite and instinct. Chrétien's stories characteristically explore the conflicts that thus arise.

Cligés

The story of *Cligés* is drawn not from Welsh legend but from classical and other sources and from oriental tales of the kind that were beginning to circulate in the West. It is directed from the start to a clear purpose, the geography is recognizable, and there are even allusions to contemporary European events. Alexander, the son and heir of the Greek emperor, goes to the court of King Arthur as to a chivalric finishing school to serve Arthur and be knighted by him. He falls in love with and marries Soredamors, who returns to Constantinople with him and their son Cligés when the emperor dies. When Cligés grows up he falls in love with Fenice, but unfortunately she is betrothed to his uncle, the usurping emperor. A plan is devised by which, after they are married, a potion will be given to the emperor that will send him to sleep every night and make him dream that he has made love to her. So Fenice will be kept inviolate. Chrétien offers this as a more honourable alternative to the adulterous love of Tristan and Isolde (p. 161), and cites St Paul in his support: 'If you cannot be pure, Saint Paul teaches you to conduct yourself with discretion' (p. 188). As often, there is a touch of irony here, but Chrétien seems certainly to have had in mind that his story might provide an ingenious moral corrective to that of Tristan and Isolde. Subsequently, Cligés, like his father, goes to Britain to win his spurs:

> In Britain, if I am bold, I can rub against the true, pure touchstone where I shall test my mettle. In Britain are to be found the worthy men acclaimed by honour and renown, and whoever wishes to gain honour must join their company, for there is honour and profit in associating with worthy men. (p. 174)

When he returns, there is more exotic plotting: Fenice feigns death by taking a trance-inducing drug, Juliet-style, and so escapes her husband and lives with Cligés in a secret tower. When the emperor gets to know of this, he goes mad with grief and dies.

Cligés is the most lavishly plotted, least enigmatic and most transparent of Chrétien's romances. There is much battling, in which Cligés succeeds all too predictably (even achieving a draw with Gawain, who is still, before the introduction of Lancelot, pre-eminent among Arthur's knights), and shows too a certain lack of finesse in charging into battle with an enemy's head already on the head of his spear. There are also more than usually lengthy soliloquies, particularly in the affair of Alexander and Soredamors, analysing the power of love, its grief and delight, its suffering and joy, the eyes which wound the heart, the arrows that pierce it, the slavery of the heart to its servant:

> Thus love tormented Fenice, but this torment was a pleasure of which she never wearied. (p. 178)

Some of these metaphors and paradoxes have perhaps become cold and formal with the passage of time and with over-use.

Yvain, ou Le Chevalier au Lion

Yvain, drawn again from Welsh legend (where Yvain is known as Owein), is perhaps the most fully satisfying of Chrétien's romances: the narrative is bold and compelling as an embodiment of Chrétien's mature reflections on the idealism of love and honour. At the beginning, to an audience comprising Guenevere, who has left Arthur asleep, and a group of knights present at the feast of Pentecost, Calogrenant recounts his defeat at the hands of the Knight of the Storm. Yvain is inspired to take up the adventure and revenge his cousin; he defeats and mortally wounds the Knight, and pursues him to the castle and in through the gate, where his horse is bisected as the portcullis comes down (Yvain's half of the horse is inside at that point). This spectacular episode was a favourite among the manuscript illustrators of the poem, whether or not because they recognized it as a representation of that fear of emasculation which is present in man when power and wealth are sought through a woman.[5] Within the castle, he falls in love with the newly widowed Laudine, and woos and wins her with the help of Lunete, her maid. Arthur arrives with his retinue and after much celebration Yvain departs with them, promising to return in a year. But he forgets his promise, and when he realizes what he has done he runs mad in the woods.

He is healed by a lady, meets with the lion, who serves him in the capacity of a squire and occasional battle-companion, and embarks on a series of adventures in which he re-proves himself as a knight, including the fight with Harpin the giant, the rescue of the three hundred oppressed maidens from the silk-factory at the castle of Pesme Aventure, and the rescue of Lunete. He meets Laudine, but does not acknowledge himself except as 'The Knight of the Lion' and keeps his identity secret until he has fully expiated his crime. This is accomplished when he fights as the champion of the wronged younger sister in a legal dispute against her older sister, who has Gawain as her champion. They fight to exhaustion, finally recognize each other, and in a spectacular contest of magnanimity each claims to have been defeated by the other. Arthur takes matters into his own hands, restores the younger sister's rights to her lands, and Yvain returns happily to Laudine, who has long forgiven him.

Yvain is full of displays of Chrétien's characteristic rhetoric. One of the high operatic moments of the poem is when, in matched scenes,

Yvain soliloquizes, with much balanced rhetoric, upon the hopelessness of loving the widow of the man he has just slain, while Laudine debates with herself whether she can love her husband's slayer. She argues herself into doing what she wants to do by pointing out to herself that Yvain cannot really be blamed since he only acted in self-defence – a touch of the legalism that Chrétien delighted in – and after all, she has a duty to marry the best knight now that her husband is dead, and clearly Yvain is the best knight, since it was he that killed him. In contemporary reality, this swift remarriage would have seemed quite practical: it is the play-acting that makes it so delightfully preposterous. Passages of internal debate like this show Chrétien's quick irony and lightness of touch, which would make embarrassing any temptation to be 'involved' in the characters' feelings in the way we are with private reading and in the novel, but rather serve to keep that 'distance' that is appropriate in reading to an assembled company of men and women.

Another purple passage elaborates the paradox of love and hate in the hearts of Yvain and Gawain when they fight against each other in ignorance of each other's identity. This is one of those rhetorically coloured and heightened pieces of writing that would have had a courtly audience murmuring with delight at the sheer bravado of it, as if they were listening to an operatic coloratura soprano, wondering whether she could bring it off without collapsing into bathos.

There are also characteristic passages in which Chrétien caters for the delight his audience had in hearing about the fashionable sophistication of the society in which they liked to think of themselves as living. An example is the passage where Chrétien describes Laudine's reception of Arthur and the knights of the Round Table. She flirts with them all in the fashionably prescribed way, making each one feel that he is in some way special, and yet requiring of each that sophistication and gentlemanly restraint that will recognize that these flirtatious attentions are not signs that she desires to be intimate with them.

> The lady so honoured him and his knights, one and all, that some fool among them might have thought that the favours and attentions she showed them came from love. But we can consider simple-minded those who believe that when a lady is polite to some poor wretch, and makes him happy and embraces him, she's in love with him. (p. 326)

All would feel amusement at this, and a glow of satisfaction at knowing they did not belong among these simple-minded fools.

But these courtly arabesques should not disguise the way Chrétien's romance provides also the testing and confirmation of chivalric values that Auerbach described as the central ethos of the romance-form. Yvain goes mad because in forgetting his promise he lost his truth, and with that he lost his integrity, his identity, his self, his reality. The rest of the poem is the story of his recovery of that truth through acts of selfless valour and concern for others. He relearns how to be a true knight, demonstrating one of the principal powers of romance-narrative, its capacity to show how human beings may be educated and transformed. What began for Yvain as 'mere adventures' has become a more serious kind of self-testing and self-proving.

One of Chrétien's great skills as a romance-writer is that he can talk about serious things without the least hint of solemnity, and central to Yvain's re-education are the intrinsically comical events involving the lion. His rescue of the lion, who is getting the worst of the battle with the dragon, despite knowing that the lion may subsequently attack him, is, as we may put it, his first act of disinterested chivalry after his recovery from madness. A true knight must always intervene on the weaker side, but it was also, we know, with that mysterious knowledge that one has in romances, simply the right thing to do. It is also the lion that brings him to a full recognition of his own loss of love and truth. Yvain accidentally stabs himself with his sword as he falls in a swoon: the lion sees the blood, thinks Yvain is dead, and prepares to die like a true Roman by falling upon the sword. This rare and possibly unique attempt at animal suicide is happily avoided by Yvain's recovery, but to Yvain it is a revelation of what love and truth mean. The whole episode transcends its potential silliness in a remarkable way: the lion is not an emblem of valour or physical prowess, but just the opposite – of Yvain's lost truth, to which he is guided back by the simplicity of the brute beast.

Romances frequently find their truest emblems of true humanity in simple creatures – in animals, in children, in servants. It is no accident that immediately following the incident with the lion, Yvain meets and makes his confession to Lunete, who serves him throughout with truth and true love. He is now given the opportunity of serving her, in the same way, with truth and true love, in rescuing her. We remember how comically awkward it is going to be next day to keep his time to rescue her when he has so many other people to rescue by 12 o'clock, but keep his time he does and explicitly makes amends for his earlier mistake. We see how far he has come from his earlier commitment to deeds of individual derring-do and revenge, and how he is moving towards the last formal statement of his resumption of his own true identity.

It would detract hardly at all from the moving power of the poem to go back and recognize that the privileging of honour and courtesy and truth over individual prowess and deeds of derring-do is a necessary and self-imposed limitation that contributes to the stability of the newly established chivalric community. In other words, if we ask why 'truth' and 'honour to women' are recommended, it is because it is a way of solidifying marital relations by shaming men into thinking of other ways of winning honour than fighting for themselves as individuals. In closing the rift between himself and Laudine, Yvain can assume a more fully productive relationship with society, as he demonstrates in the long process of winning reconcilement.[6]

Perceval, ou Le Conte du Graal, and its Continuations

In the last of his romances, the unfinished *Perceval,* or *Le Conte du Graal* ('The Story of the Grail'), Chrétien introduced the Grail, the Bleeding Lance and the Fisher King for the first time into Arthurian romance. They are associated with a quest, and with a symbolic Christian meaning, though this is as yet only hinted at. They were to provide rich material for more explicitly Christian development in the works of the continuators of the *Conte* and the compilers of the vast cyclic prose Arthurian romances of the thirteenth century.

Perceval is brought up in isolation in the Welsh woods by his mother, in ignorance of his lineage since she does not want him killed like her husband and two other sons. But he needs only the sight of a group of knights to be stirred to emulation, and he leaves home, rudely clad and ill provided, to become a knight. Instinctively he has all the fighting skills, and he quickly becomes adept in them, though the acquisition of the refinements of behaviour, in this comical rehearsal of a chivalric education, take longer. After being knighted by Arthur, he determines to return and see his mother, but he is constantly distracted by adventures that spring up. At the castle of the Fisher King (p. 421) he sees a white lance with blood dripping from its tip and a grail, or serving-dish, borne through the hall but not used. Nothing is explained, and Perceval does not ask. Later, he learns that the Fisher King is so called because, being wounded in both thighs and incapable of walking or riding, he goes fishing in a boat for pastime, and he learns too that his silence in the face of the grail and the lance will bring waste and disaster to the land. His wretchedness in failing to ask the question is his punishment for not having returned to his mother, who has now died. Much later, he is told that the use of the grail is to carry the host daily to the Fisher King's father, as the sustenance that alone keeps him alive. The lance is not explained, but a spiritual meaning, in relation to the blood of Christ, seems to be implied, and is suggested in a beautiful later passage (p. 432) where Perceval grows lost in contemplation of three drops of blood upon the snow, while all around him the daily business of challenging and fighting goes on unnoticed.

At the midpoint of the poem's 9000 lines, a series of quests is inaugurated at Arthur's court, including that of Perceval, who will not rest till he finds the meaning of the grail and the bleeding lance, and that of Gawain, who will rescue the maiden besieged at Montesclere. Gawain's miscellaneous adventures with the Bed of Marvels and the Perilous Ford and at the castle of the Rock of Champguin, where he unexpectedly finds himself sitting next to both Arthur's mother and his own, are recounted in luxuriant detail, without achieving any clear direction. Perceval's quest receives only 200 lines: he loses faith, meets some penitents on Good Friday who expound to him succinctly the meaning of Christ's sacrifice (p. 458), and goes to a hermit from whom he hears the explanation of the grail and from whom he himself receives communion. At this point Chrétien says:

> The tale no longer speaks of Perceval at this point; you will have heard
> a great deal about my lord Gawain before I speak of Perceval again.
> (p. 461)

In fact, no more is heard of him before the poem breaks off unfinished in mid-sentence.

It is all very mysterious. The enigmas and mysteriousness of *Lancelot* look transparent beside this profound riddling, which is both exasperating and irresistible. It is hard to know what Chrétien's purpose was, if he had one, but a contrast seems to be being developed between Perceval and Gawain. Perceval begins with an almost lunatic single-mindedness in pursuing what he understands to be the ideal of knighthood, pure prowess, but is gradually civilized into a fuller understanding of the ideals of chivalry. The castle of the Fisher King is his epiphany, an unintelligible experience of great significance that must be continually revisited and meditated upon. The Unasked Question is explained, after a fashion, but it has a deeper meaning in relation to the question Perceval is being led to about the conduct of his life. He acquires a meditative self, as in the trance he falls into at the contemplation of the drops of blood in the snow, which is reminiscent of Lancelot's similar quasi-religious experiences (both are nearly killed by unnoticed assailants) but which clearly prepares for a different kind of revelation – that the life of the knight is perfected in the service of Christ. Gawain, by contrast, has old-fashioned adventures, in which he is much led by events. Without behaving badly or licentiously, he seems impressionable, and lacking in singleness of purpose. He is already on the slopes of his future decline into the playboy of Arthur's court. Arthur himself, meanwhile, is benign and distant, unfailingly courteous, but seemingly left behind by events.

The unfinishedness of Chrétien's *Perceval* is perhaps not greatly to its disadvantage. The suspendedness of the narrative, the meanings hinted at in the parallel quests of Perceval and Gawain, the mysteries only half-revealed, are part of its hold on the reader. As Frappier says, Chrétien often retains 'the inconsequences and extravagances' of his Celtic originals 'in order to pique the curiosity of his readers by an enigma or to startle them with a surprise . . . He was not insensible to the charm of this mythology in ruins'.[7] In the four continuations and their variant versions, some of them much longer than the original, the prolongation of the two heroes' adventures involves some laborious tying up of loose ends and the addition of many episodes of a routinely repetitive rather than mysteriously significant nature. The First Continuation is devoted to Gawain: he makes his own visit to the Grail-castle and embarks on the quest, but it seems to make no difference to his conduct or his outlook on life. The Second Continuation, by Wauchier de Denain, continues by following the adventures of both heroes, but breaks off as Perceval enters the Grail-castle. The Third and Fourth Continuations, completed some thirty years later, in the 1220s, both follow on from the Second and are heavily didactic and Christianized. In the former, Perceval eventually completes the Grail quest, slays Partinial, heals the Fisher King and restores his land, where Perceval later reigns before retiring to a hermitage to spend his last ten years sustained by the Grail alone. In the Fourth Continuation, by Gerbert de Montreuil, Perceval defeats Tristan (who had by now emerged as an important knight of the Round Table) and all of Arthur's knights at a tournament organized by King Mark of Cornwall, vows himself to virginity on the night of his wedding to Blancheflor (whom he first met in the *Perceval*), and likewise eventually achieves the Grail. The Bleeding Lance is finally explained as the lance with which Longinus pierced Christ's side, and the Grail as the dish used by Joseph of Arimathaea to catch Christ's blood. There is also now a Broken Sword – the one with which the Fisher King wounded himself in his grief at the death of his brother, slain by the traitor Partinial. The reuniting of the two parts of the sword is another task of the successful Grail-knight.

3

The European Flourishing of Arthurian Romance: Lancelot, Parzival, Tristan

French Arthurian Romance in Verse and Prose

The continuations of Chrétien's *Perceval*, or *Conte du Graal*, already give evidence of the inexhaustible appetite of late twelfth- and early thirteenth-century audiences for Arthurian romances of chivalric adventures and quests laced with love-interest and religious significance. Many such romances were written, particularly in France, to satisfy fashionable taste among an increasing leisured class of listeners and readers.

Among those who composed in verse was Robert de Boron, of whose three poems, *Joseph d'Arimathie*, *Merlin* and *Perceval*, only the first (written *c*.1200) and a fragment of the second survive. In *Joseph d'Arimathie*, he identified the Grail for the first time with the cup that Christ used at the Last Supper. This cup was given afterwards to Pilate, and then to Joseph of Arimathaea, who gathered in it the last drops of Christ's blood at the Deposition. Joseph set up a service of the Grail, in memory of the Last Supper, to which only the pure might be summoned. Later, the Grail is carried west to the 'vaus d'Avaron', where it is to await the coming of a descendant of Joseph of Arimathaea. The valley of Avaron is to be identified as the flatlands surrounding Glastonbury, where the abbey already had strong associations with Arthur: his remains were famously exhumed there in 1191.

Robert de Boron's poem is remote from Arthurian tradition, attached only through the symbolism of the Grail, first adumbrated in Chrétien, but his work, including that which he tells us about but which does not now survive, was to have considerable further influence. He represents a clericalization of Arthurian romance which was to become more and more powerful.

At the opposite end of the Arthurian spectrum of the spiritual and the profane, as it was marked out by Chrétien, was Gawain (Gauvain), the hero of a number of early verse romances. From being the first among Arthur's knights, renowned for his courage and prowess, he declines, because of the promotion, for different reasons, of Lancelot, Perceval and Tristan, into a knight more famous for his courtesy and frequently improper service to women, and at worst a womanizer often involved in slightly comic adventures and misadventures. In *Le Chevalier à l'Epée* ('The Knight with the Sword'), for instance, written before 1200, he receives a familiar invitation – to sleep with his host's daughter – knowing that there is danger involved. Nevertheless, he cannot resist making love to her, but just as he is about to achieve what the romances call the 'soreplus', the maiden warns him urgently to beware.[1] Feeling that his reputation as a ladies' man is at stake, he carries on, but immediately mysterious swords are flying about in all directions, just missing or slightly wounding him, and his ardour is cooled. This happens more than once, and next morning he is able to proclaim his innocence and, having involuntarily passed the test, he receives the girl in marriage as his prize. Taking her back to Arthur's court, he meets a knight who attempts to seize his bride-to-be. Gawain, embarrassingly, is not equipped for battle, and it is suggested that the lady should choose between them. Much to his chagrin, and with some sardonic remarks about Gawain's 'prowess', she prepares to ride off with the total stranger. Gawain explodes in a violent outburst against women. There is more of this story, none of it much to Gawain's credit.

Gawain is the 'hero' also of another short verse romance of about 1200, *La Mule sans Frein* ('The Mule without a Bridle'), where he has adventures and misfortunes of a more crudely comic nature, though without completely forfeiting the status that he must have if the comedy is not to lose its edge. In Raoul de Houdenc's *La Vengeance Raguidel*, a full-length verse romance of about 1220, Gawain has a similarly ambiguous role. The adventures in which he is involved often place him in dilemmas from which it is impossible to escape without loss of dignity. He becomes something of a scapegoat for the failings of chivalry to live up to its high idealism. The persistence of verse in these Gawain-romances, even though it was no longer fashionable in aristocratic reading circles, is perhaps the mark of an appeal to a slightly less refined audience.

Verse romances are generally associated with a primary listening audience. Prose romance, especially when it is presented in handsome manuscripts with pictures, seems to be more appropriate to a reading audience. Such manuscripts begin to be produced early in the thirteenth century, and over a hundred survive: the earliest illustrated prose *Lancelot* may be Rennes, Bibliothèque Municipale MS 255, made in Paris (*c.*1220–30) and associated with the royal court. Manuscripts of this kind soon got to be very large and splendid, with many pictures, though with generalized scenes (of combat, siege, procession, meeting) rather than scenes adapted to specific episodes – a sign of the pressures of mass production.

Arthurian romance, in verse and prose, swept Europe, and a form so fashionable could not escape clerical appropriation, especially in its prose forms. An early example is the vast prose Grail-romance of *Perlesvaus* (a scribal variant of the name 'Perceval'), composed soon after 1200. Its aim is thoroughly to appropriate Arthurian romance to the purposes of religion by making the Grail the essential goal of the knightly quest and the symbol of a new life of Christian purity. Arthur wins his way to a remote Welsh chapel, where an old hermit tells him that the decline of the Round Table, stemming from Perceval's Unasked Question, can only be reversed through the quest of the Grail. This is undertaken in turn by Gawain, who reaches the castle of the Fisher King but fails to ask the question because he becomes distracted by the spectacle; by Lancelot, who also fails, though extolled as the ideal of knighthood; and by Perceval, who finds the Fisher King dead, so that the expected question is never asked (though we are by now pretty clear about the likely answer). He retires from the world to become a hermit after further episodes in which Lancelot and then Arthur and Gawain go to Avalon (Glastonbury) to visit the tomb of Guenevere, who has died of grief after the death of her son Loholt. There is elaborate cross-referencing to earlier romances throughout *Perlesvaus*, and the beginnings of fully cyclic interlaced narration.

Another example of clericalized prose romance is the *Didot Perceval*, so called after an early owner of the first manuscript, and written not long after 1200. It is based on the lost *Perceval* of Robert de Boron, as is deduced from the similarity of its contents to Robert's summary of his own *Perceval* at the end of *Joseph d'Arimathie*. Perceval is now recognized as the grandson of Joseph of Arimathaea's brother Bron, and thus the destined true Grail-knight. He goes to Arthur's court to be knighted, and rashly takes his seat in the stone Siege Perilous, which splits beneath him with a great roar. A voice proclaims that the stone seat will never be mended until a knight who surpasses all others in virtue goes to the Grail-castle to ask what the Grail is and who is served with it. Perceval makes an unsuccessful visit to the Grail-castle, more or less repeating the experience described in Chrétien, and is much engaged in other adventures, including the ever-recurring quest of the White Hart. At last he returns to the Grail-castle, asks the Question, and the Fisher King, who turns out to be his grandfather Bron, explains its mysteries to him, entrusts him with the vessel, and dies. The Siege Perilous is made whole, and Merlin announces to Arthur the fulfilment of the Grail quest.

The *Didot Perceval* is associated in some manuscripts with a prose romance of *Merlin*, based again on Robert de Boron, and recounting Merlin's prophecies and his part in Arthur's early career; and also with a *Mort d'Artu* ('Death of Arthur'), which tells the familiar story of Arthur's conquest of Gaul, his return to face the Roman envoys, his continental campaign, Mordred's treason, and Arthur's departure to Avalon to be cured of his wound. There was already in shadowy existence, it appears, a coherent cycle of Arthurian romances, covering events from the death of Christ to Arthur's last battle, though not exactly in the manner that Geoffrey of Monmouth or Chrétien de Troyes might have anticipated.

The Vulgate Cycle of Arthurian Romances

Subsequently, a number of authors and compilers, working *c.*1215–30 under the spiritual direction or influence or inspiration of Cistercian monastic teaching, gathered the sprawling mass of stories into a single vast, broadly chronological cycle known as the 'Vulgate' cycle (because in French not in Latin) of Arthurian prose romance. It survives in many forms and many manuscripts, and occupies seven large quarto volumes in the only edition that aims at completeness. The nucleus was the magnificent *Lancelot* (*c.*1215–30, the one that appears in the illustrated manuscripts mentioned above), the story of which was continued in the *Queste del Saint Graal* (the story of the quest for the Grail by the knights of the Round Table, with Galahad now the destined Grail-knight, and Perceval and Bohort the runners-up) and concluded in the *Mort Artu* (the story of the death of Arthur). The whole of this sequence is often now known as the 'Lancelot-Graal cycle'. Prefixed to the *Lancelot*, as a retrospective prequel, was an account of the early history of the Grail (the *Estoire del Saint Graal*, how the chalice that had contained Christ's blood was brought to England by Joseph of Arimathaea), partly derived from Robert de Boron, and the story of Merlin (the *Estoire de Merlin*). The latter, partly derived from Robert de Boron's lost *Merlin*, tells of Merlin's strange birth, of the magical manoeuvrings through which he brings Arthur to the throne, and of his early interventions to help Arthur in his battles against the British warlords and the Saxon invaders. This fills in a gap in Arthur's career after his coronation. There is also for the first time the story of Merlin's fatal love for the enchantress Viviane. Otherwise, Merlin is a creature of puckish spirit, full of pranks and mystifications that annoy the reader almost as much as those he practises upon. Merlin is associated with the introduction of the Round Table, which is carefully linked with the Grail story, being a replica of the table fashioned by Joseph of Arimathaea for the first Grail ceremony and in its turn modelled on the table of the Last Supper.

Later, the extensively expanded legend of Tristan, from a completely different set of sources, with the loosest connection with Arthur, was added (*c*.1225–35), adapted into prose as *Le Roman de Tristan de Léonois* on the model of the Vulgate cycle. It survives in many manuscripts. It provided an anticipatory sub-plot, with another cuckolded king, for the doomed love-affair of Lancelot and Guenevere (Guenièvre), but it is in most respects a vulgarization of the story told in verse by Gottfried von Strassburg and his French predecessors. The tragic and irresolvable conflict in which Tristan must be untrue to his overlord King Mark because of his fated love for Queen Iseult is reduced to a simple black-and-white opposition: Mark is not a noble and wronged and bewildered king but a villain and a traitor, and an enemy of Arthurian knighthood. It is almost Tristan's duty to steal his wife. Towards the end, after he has introduced the second Iseult, 'Iseult of the White Hands', the compiler abandons the poignant continuation of the story and has Tristan embark on a series of fantastic adventures in which he eventually qualifies to become a knight of the Round Table. At the end, Tristan is simply murdered by King Mark as he sits playing his harp to Queen Iseult. It seems that the compiler was throughout more concerned to strengthen the Arthurian flavour of the romance than to attend to its special character as a story. It is a great pity that it was this version of the Tristan story that was used by both Malory and Tennyson, and not the version found in the earlier French and German poems.

The cycle as a whole was reshaped around 1230–40, with a still more extended role for Merlin in the *Suite du Merlin*, and in truth it would be idle to pretend that it ever had an 'existence' as a fixed and coherent work, variations from which could be analysed and classified. Such has been an implied assumption of some earlier scholarship, working with models derived from the technologies of print and the taxonomies of science, but the evidence is not easily assembled to bear it out.

The central purpose of the compilers of the Vulgate cycle is most evident in the incorporation of the Grail story as an integral element in the larger narrative, with a significance given to the Grail itself which was anticipated in the continuators and imitators of Chrétien. In the unfinished poem of *Perceval* or *Le Conte du Graal* attributed to Chrétien, the Grail is a vaguely mysterious object connected with a maimed Fisher King who will be healed when he is asked what the Grail is for. Already at this point all the features of the story so resonant with archetypal implication for Jessie L. Weston and, following her, for T. S. Eliot are there – the Waste Land, the Fisher King, the Hidden Castle with its Solemn Feast, the mysterious Feeding Vessel, the Bleeding Lance and the Cup.[2] But in the Vulgate cycle, following the romances associated with Robert de Boron, the Grail became the object of a quest for spiritual perfection in which the Knights of the Round Table could not but fail, because of their investment in the world and in women, and in which a new hero had to be invented who would win it, Galahad (Galaad), son of Lancelot. Galahad wins the Grail and therefore leaves the fellowship. The failure of the knights of the Round Table in the Grail quest was the demonstration of the irredeemably fallen state of secular chivalry. Where individual writers might see at times in the story of Lancelot and Guenevere a human meaningfulness, even a tragic conflict of high ideals of love and honour, the Vulgate compilers, inspired by ascetic and other-worldly

ideals, saw principally a lesson to be learnt concerning the nothingness of worldly desire. At the end, the deaths of Arthur, Lancelot and
Guenevere are enclosed in consoling pieties; Guenevere ends up in a
nunnery and Lancelot in a monastery and both explicitly repudiate
worldly love.

But these large strategies of appropriation, though they may attempt to redirect the narrative towards different goals, cannot change
its essential nature as the record of the whole life of adventure taken
up in the cause of love and chivalry. The vast expanses of the cycle,
encompassing the exploits of scores of named knights, have a complexity, an irresolution, that make them resistant to a single interpretation. Characters appear, disappear and reappear, story-lines cross,
run parallel, loop around each other, and are sometimes suspended
for long periods. The narrative technique of *entrelacement* ('interlac-
ing'), 'in which one episode is interrupted by another, which in turn
is broken off in order to continue the earlier narrative',[3] ensures that
something exciting is always happening or about to happen, but the
technique resists closure, and characters are typically entwined in
endless repetitions – Lancelot is always in love with Guenevere, always going away, always coming back; Tristan is always in love with
Isolde (one or the other), always going away, always coming back;
Palamides is always in pursuit of the mysterious *beste glatissant* ('bark-
ing beast'). There are endless single combats, conducted according to
a set pattern, as strict as the steps of a dance. When any two knights
meet in the forest, in no time they will have fewtered their spears
and hurled together like thunder so strongly that both their horses
will be rashed to the earth. Then they will avoid their saddles and
dress their shields and draw their swords and fling together as wood
men or lash together with great strokes and foin like two bulls or wild
boars and give many strokes, maybe fight for two hours, until one
gives the other such a buffet that he kneels on his knees, whereupon
the first, who is usually Sir Lancelot, will unlace the helm of the
defeated knight and threaten to strike off his head unless he will
agree that Guenevere is the fairest of all ladies.[4] If the defeated com-
batant is lucky, that is, for otherwise he will not even get the chance
to do this because he will already have been cloven to the shoulder or
the navel or some other final-sounding part of his anatomy.

The great narrative achievement of the prose *Lancelot*, and of the
much shorter *Queste* and *Mort Artu*, which are integral as sequels, is to

make Lancelot the convincingly central protagonist of the whole story, with Arthur now a subordinate figure. Even as the story draws to its close in the *Mort Artu*, the magnificent climax to the whole cycle, it is Lancelot who holds centre-stage: his rescue of Guenevere from the stake after Agravain's accusations of adultery prompts the long wars against Arthur and Gawain, which play a much more important part than Arthur's continental campaigns against the Romans, and after the last battle Lancelot returns to England to avenge Arthur's death before retiring to a hermitage. It is he whose soul is last seen, flying skyward.

Lancelot is the greatest of all knights, by far, greatest in prowess, courtesy and honour, and thus his failure to win the Grail is a powerful indictment of the world of secular chivalry. Yet Lancelot is also the father of Galahad, begotten upon the Grail King's daughter, whom he mistakenly thinks to be Guenevere. We learn in the opening sentences of the *Lancelot* that Lancelot himself was called Galahad in baptism, one of many significant foreshadowings through which the great arch of destiny is projected upon the old mysterious incoherences of the story. Everything, in this reading of the story, has the potential of becoming profoundly meaningful, and Lancelot embodies in himself both the highest aspirations of the worldly knight and the tragic failure of the messianic ambition. Lesser weaknesses are scored out so that the higher weakness will appear more stark. The first consummation of Lancelot's love for Guenevere, for instance, takes place on the night that Arthur is in bed with the enchantress Camille, Lancelot's adultery being thus in some way made to seem less heinous. The episode of the cart (Chrétien's narrative is still being extensively plundered) is purged of every ignominious and ironically comic association. Yet with all this skill in narrative shaping and rationalization, and the careful apparatus of omen and prophecy and advancing doom, the vast expanses of the *Lancelot* remain a territory where every reader feels, most of the time, pleasurably at a loss to know exactly what is happening. Only at the end, as Chrétien's story of Lancelot's love for Guenevere is blended into Geoffrey of Monmouth's story of the downfall of Arthur through the treachery of Mordred, does the narrative fully acquire the impetus and coherent motivation that modern readers assume to be the essentials of good story-telling. It is in the *Mort Artu* that we find for the first time the superb closing scene of the casting of the sword

Escalibor (Excalibur) into the lake and the repeated hesitations of Giflet (Bedivere in Malory) before he finally obeys. Only at the very end, with the cloistering and death of Lancelot and Guenevere, are the Cistercian pieties reasserted.

It is possible to accept that there are several different hands at work in the Vulgate cycle, but the overarching continuity of the story of Lancelot through the *Lancelot*, the *Queste* and the *Mort Artu*, and the brilliant stroke of invention by which Galahad is introduced as his son, suggest that the conception as a whole was the work of a single 'architect', as Frappier calls him.[5] The prose *Lancelot* is one of the great literary achievements of the Middle Ages, and Dante recognized this in singling it out as the instrument of eternal perdition for Paolo and Francesca, who seal their fate with their first kiss as they read together of the first love-kiss of Lancelot and Guenevere.[6]

It is not surprising that the world of medieval Arthurian love-romance, so massively present in these narrative cycles and their derivatives and descendants (which include, in England, Sir Thomas Malory's *Morte D'Arthur* of *c.*1470), has proved such an enduring legacy, and provided such a wealth of stories, themes and images and such a cast of characters for later enjoyment and exploitation. There is no way in which this resource can be 'used up'.

Arthurian Romance in Europe

French Arthurian romance spread throughout Europe. The tastes of the French-speaking aristocracy of Flanders and Brabant, like that of England, were mostly well satisfied by French versions of Arthurian romance, but there are Middle Dutch renderings of Arthurian romance, as early as the thirteenth century, that are evidently designed for an aspirant bourgeoisie, much like the contemporary English versions of French romance. They survive in simpler manuscripts, with fewer miniatures, and are less interested in fine points of courtly behaviour and sentiment than in broadly playful treatments of Arthurian subject-matter. Gawain, by now commonly the unheroic hero of slightly comic adventures with women, is a favourite character: in an interpolation in the Middle Dutch version of the prose *Lancelot* he is transformed into a midget lover so that he can find out the true nature of his mistress Ydain.

In addition to Arthurian romances, there are of course also many chivalric love-romances newly based on classical, Celtic, oriental and other originals. But the inheritance of chivalric love-romance is dominated, in Europe generally as in England and Germany, by Arthurian story. There are translations and adaptations in prose and verse of the romances of Chrétien and the Vulgate cycle in Spain, Portugal and Italy, and frequent familiar reference to the persons and events of the story in art as well as literature. The most striking witness to the widespread diffusion of Arthurian romance is in Norway and Iceland, where, side by side with the flourishing of the most vigorous indigenous saga-tradition in Europe (rivalled perhaps only by Ireland), there are also thirteenth-century translations into the prose of the sagas of some of the most important French Arthurian verse romances, including *Ivens saga*, *Erex saga* and *Parcevals saga*, all based on Chrétien. There are also adaptations of Thomas's *Tristan* and of two of Marie de France's *lais*, but no translation of any of the romances from the prose cycles.

Subjects from Arthurian romance were also favourites throughout Europe in all forms of interior decoration, furnishings and *objets d'art*. One of the most famous single pieces of medieval goldsmithing is a salt-cellar belonging to Louis, first duke of Anjou (d. 1384), depicting the episode in the story of Tristan in which King Mark, up in a tree, eavesdrops upon the lovers, who have been forewarned of his presence. The incident was often selected for representation: in a single image it seems to capture the complexity of motive and emotional sympathy at the heart of the romance, where the wronged king does something mean-spirited and degrading to find out the truth, and the lovers play clever tricks to deceive him further. It was a good subject for dinner-table conversation.

Elsewhere, well-preserved wall-paintings at the castles of Rodenegg in the south Tyrol (*c.*1225) and Schmalkalden in Thuringia (*c.*1230) tell the story of Yvain, hero of the romance by Chrétien de Troyes (if 'hero' is the right word for a knight who completely forgets his promise to return to his wife within a year and who has to perform a prolonged chivalric penance in order to be restored to her favour). Such paintings focus the story as a series of images, acting as a visual reminder for those who know the story and perhaps adding something of their own, for a picture is rarely a simple pictorial 'equivalent' of a text. One of the favourite subjects for illustration in manuscripts of

Yvain is the episode, already mentioned, in which Yvain, riding in hot pursuit of a knight whom he has fatally wounded (the knight is the husband of the lady that Yvain proceeds immediately to woo and win), follows him through the castle-gate and has his horse cut off just behind the saddle by the descending portcullis. What thoughts might this bizarre illustration have provoked, beyond what is suggested in the text, of the male sovereignties that were put at risk in such a marriage?

Arthurian Romance in Germany

German courtly culture reached a high degree of sophistication, partly under French influence, in the princely and episcopal courts of Bamberg, Cologne, Eisenach, Mainz, Naumberg, Nürnberg, Regensburg, Strassburg and Würzburg, during the reigns of the Hohenstaufen emperors Frederick I (1152–90), Henry VI (1190–7) and Frederick II (1218–50). The material appurtenances of courtly culture (castles, clothes, food, weapons) became more elegant and expensive, courtly feasts and other ceremonial occasions such as tournaments became more grand, and the cultivation of courtly ideals of knighthood, woman-liness, love and eroticized religion, and the representation of those ideals by the poets, became more extravagant and self-conscious.

The earliest Arthurian romances in the language known as Middle High German are the verse translations of Chrétien de Troyes by Hartmann von Aue, whose *Erek* (*c.*1190) and *Iwein* (*c.*1202) are inspired by high ideals of courtly conduct and sometimes primly resistant to Chrétien's irony. In *Erek*, the German poet works freely and invent-ively with Chrétien, who is not his only source, tending specially, for instance, to exaggerate moments of crisis and high drama, like Enite's grief over Erek's apparently lifeless body, which Chrétien treats in a more detached manner. In *Iwein*, there is more of a hammering home of the theme of education and expiation which it is the reader's pleasure in Chrétien's poem to feel has been uncovered in the process of reading.

At the same time that Hartmann von Aue was writing, or rather while he was off on Crusade (1193–7), there also appeared a German verse romance of *Lanzelet* (*c.*1195) translated from an Anglo-Norman original of about 1180 by the Swiss priest Ulrich von Zatzikhoven. He tells us he acquired the French book from Hugh de Morville, one of the hostages for his own release sent by Richard Lion-heart to Duke Leopold of Austria and later transferred to the court of the emperor Henry VI. The poem is not a translation of Chrétien's *Lancelot*: the only point of comparison is the episode in which Lanzelet fights as the champion of Queen Ginover against her abductor Valerin. Both authors may have drawn on common legendary material, but the development of the relationship of Lancelot and Guenevere is all Chrétien's. For the rest, *Lanzelet* tells of the hero's childhood, carried off by a water-fairy and brought up among women in ignorance of his royal birth (some of this material was later incorporated into the prose *Lancelot*), and of his serial conquests of the hearts of neighbouring princesses before he is welcomed at Arthur's court, fights for Ginover, loves and deserts another queen, restores a maiden who has been transformed into a dragon by kissing it (her) on the lips, and finally returns home to his kingdom with the lady Iblis, one of his early conquests whom he seems inadvertently to have married some time ago.

The contrast between this crude potboiler and the *Parzival* (*c.*1210) of Wolfram von Eschenbach, a free translation, with much added material, of Chrétien's *Perceval*, could hardly be greater. One of the masterpieces of medieval Arthurian romance, it gives focus to the sprawling French work by the use of thematic anticipation and echo, by offering motivation to seemingly random episodes, by introducing an idealized lady, Sigune, who figures symbolically at key moments in the hero's Grail quest, and by making explicit the contrast between Gawan (Gawain), the paragon of courtly conduct, and Parzival, in whom the courtly code is identical with the life dedicated to God. There is a strong emphasis on religious and ethical teaching, and Wolfram turns aside completely from Chrétien's story in his Book IX to take his hero on a visit to the hermit Trevrizent, who explains the true meaning of the Grail as the 'stone of humility'. Wolfram also provides an ending for the story in which Parzival is admitted by the guardians of the Holy Grail at Munsalväsche ('the mount of Salvation') and crowned King of the Grail with his wife Condwiramurs and his son Loherangrin. If there is, in medieval Arthurian romance, a spectrum running from amorous libertinism to high eroticized spiritual devotion, Parzival is at the extreme latter end.

Gottfried von Strassburg, *Tristan*

Gottfried von Strassburg's *Tristan*, also written about 1210, is likewise suffused with the sentiment and language of piety, but in a manner hinting always at irreverence. It is a highly sophisticated work, full of ironic and other tricks of narration that look back to Chrétien and forward to Chaucer. It is all something of a surprise to those whose image of a medieval German court is of draughty windowless castles, stone floors, animal skin rugs, beer-swilling thugs and clanging iron-mongery. Gottfried was a well-educated member of the urban patriciate of Strassburg, one of the largest cities of Hohenstaufen Germany, and probably either a 'ministerial' (like Chaucer) or an episcopal official. His version of the Tristan story is derived from the *Tristran* of Thomas (of which only fragments survive), composed probably for Eleanor of Aquitaine about 1160, one of two major twelfth-century French versions of the Tristan story. The other, by Béroul (*c.*1170), represents the older version of the story that came down in the prose *Tristan*. Though only the last sixth of Thomas's poem survives, its story can be reconstructed from the various other poems that were explicitly indebted to it, including Gottfried's, and it is clear that it was in Thomas that the elaborate dialectic and ambiguous morality of the high code of love, whether or not under the inspiration of Queen Eleanor, were first infused into the story. It was a poem that caught the mood of the moment. By a surprising coincidence, the surviving text of Thomas begins almost exactly where that of Gottfried breaks off. As for Arthur, he is briefly mentioned in Thomas for his giant-slaying exploits, and following him in Gottfried, at the beginning of Chapter 31, but otherwise not at all.

Gottfried begins with a statement of his primary purpose – to write for those who are expert in love's sorrows, an elite of the melancholy.

> 'I do not mean', he says, 'the world of the many who (as I hear) are unable to endure sorrow and wish only to revel in bliss . . . I have another world in mind which together in one heart bears its bitter-sweet, its dear sorrow, its heart's joy, its love's pain, its dear life, its sorrowful death, its dear death, its sorrowful life. To this life let my life be given, of this world let me be part, to be damned or saved with it.'
> (translation, p. 42)

His work will help those who are sorrowful in love by occupying their thoughts with the sorrows of others. Nevertheless, love's sorrow is a sorrow to be cherished – 'This sorrow is so full of joy, this ill so inspiriting that, having once been heartened by it, no noble heart will forgo it' (p. 42). Gottfried offers the classic statement of the importance of love and its dwelling only in noble hearts – 'Love is so blissful a thing, so blessed an endeavour, that apart from its teaching none attains worth or reputation' (p. 43). The sorrow and joy of Tristan and Isolde in love is what nourishes those who read it. As the priest intones the liturgy before offering the bread of the eucharistic sacrifice – 'I am the living bread . . . If any man eat of this bread he shall live for ever; and the bread that I give is my flesh, which I shall give for the life of the world' – so Gottfried intones the liturgy of his Prologue before offering the bread of the lovers' sacrifice in the form of his story, which will give life to noble lovers.

> This is bread to all noble hearts. With this their death lives on. We read their life, we read their death, and to us it is sweet as bread. Their life, their death are our bread. Thus lives their life, thus lives their death. Thus they live still and yet are dead, and their death is the bread of the living. (p. 44)

> Deist aller edelen herzen brôt.
> hie mite sô lebet ir beider tôt.
> wir lesen ir leben, wir lesen ir tôt:
> und ist uns daz süez' alse brôt.
> Ir leben, ir tôt sint unser brôt.
> sus lebet ir leben, sus lebet ir tôt.
> sus lebent si noch und sint doch tôt.
> und ist ir tôt der lebenden brôt.
> (lines 233–40)

The poem begins in Brittany with the torments and joys of the love of Rivalin and Blancheflor, the sister of King Mark of Cornwall. Tristan is conceived in what at first seems to be a dying embrace, as Rivalin, badly wounded in battle, nearly overstrains himself when Blancheflor comes to his bed: 'As to Rivalin, he was all but dead, both of the woman and love' (p. 58). But soon enough they are both dead, and Tristan left an orphan. Inevitably, he is called Tristan:

His name came from 'triste'. The name was well suited to him, and in every way appropriate. Let us test it by the story, let us see how full of sorrow it was when his mother was delivered of him, see how soon trouble and pain were loaded upon him, see what a sorrowful life he was given to live, see the sorrowful death that brought his anguish to a close with an end beyond comparison of all deaths, more bitter than all sorrow. (pp. 67–8)

Gottfried comes close here to speaking of Tristan's life as a martyrdom for the sake of love, and of course there is more than an echo of Christ as the man of sorrows who shed his blood for love (literally true in the bloodletting scene, which we shall hear of later). These daring allusive meanings are all part of Gottfried's strategy of going to the brink of what contemporary sensibility will permit, and maybe just beyond, as well as fulfilling an important function as dramatic irony, or prefiguration.

Tristan finds his way to Cornwall, where he becomes Mark's favourite even before his parentage is revealed. He is declared Mark's heir, and is chosen as a champion against Morold, brother of Queen Isolde of Ireland, who has come for the tribute of sons, and kills him in single combat. A portion of Tristan's sword stuck in Morold's head is dug out by the queen and her daughter, also called Isolde, when his remains are returned to Ireland. But Tristan is wounded in the groin and goes alone to Ireland as a minstrel (Tantris) to be healed by Queen Isolde, who has something of a medical reputation (and a very beautiful daughter). As he recovers, he tutors Princess Isolde in music and other matters and so raves about her on his return that Mark's advisers, who are jealous of Tristan's rise, persuade Mark to seek her in marriage so that he will get a proper heir and exclude Tristan. Tristan is put in charge of the wooing expedition. The delicate problem of ingratiating himself with Morold's family, as Tristan now and not as Tantris, is managed by Tristan with some skill.

He returns with Isolde to King Mark. She is still not best pleased with Tristan, her uncle's slayer. But the love-potion, accidentally given to them on the boat when Isolde's faithful servant Brangane is absent, changes all this. They vow their love, and hatch a plot to substitute Brangane, since she is still a virgin, on the wedding night. They continue thus happily and satisfactorily painfully in their secret liaison, helped by the close kinship of Mark and Tristan, 'with which they trafficked dishonestly and won their sport by cheating' (p. 212).

Marjodoc, Tristan's friend and Mark's steward, finds the lovers in bed, and warns Mark of his suspicions. Mark does nothing, but the plots of the dwarf Melot are more successful, and Tristan is banished from the ladies' quarters.

Now comes a series of most elaborate stratagems. First, Mark, informed by his spies, hides in a tree to watch them meet beside the brook (the episode alluded to in the table decoration mentioned already), but they are forewarned by the shadows and speak an elaborately devious dialogue concerning her mediation with Mark for Tristan. This, one of the most famous scenes of voyeurism in literature, is commonly talked about in terms of prurience, concealment and the oppressive surveillance of the male gaze, but it seems more pathetic than sinister, with Mark apparently determined to find out what he doesn't want to know (compare Othello's demand that Iago supply 'ocular proof'). It is also, though, more subtly, a fulfilment of his deepest desire, which is the creation of intimacy with the lovers, both of them, through the manipulation of distance: there are for him, in the tree, as he thinks, no obstacles to the fantasy of closeness, the fantasy of access to the secret other life, a 'true' one.

Then there is the stratagem of the bloodletting scene. Tristan, having been bled companionably in the same room as Isolde, tries to leap from his recovery-bed to hers (to avoid stepping in the flour that King Mark has had spread on the floor to detect any impropriety) and bursts open all his veins and fills her bed with blood. If this seems outrageous, Gottfried has more. Isolde, faced with the ordeal of the red-hot iron when the truth of her story about the incriminating evidence of the bedful of blood is to be tested, must endeavour to make her oath of chastity truthful by a trick: Tristan, disguised as an old pilgrim, shall carry her across a ford and, when he falls over and she falls on top of him, she can swear this oath truthfully to King Mark:

> 'That no man in the world had carnal knowledge of me or lay in my arms or beside me but you, always excepting the poor pilgrim whom, with your own eyes, you saw lying in my arms.' (p. 248)

All normal morality seems dubiously suspended here, and further in the recounting of Isolde's negotiations with Christ for the success of her master-plan:

> She feared for her honour and she was harassed by the secret anxiety
> that she would have to whitewash her falseness. With these two cares
> she did not know what to do: she confided them to Christ, the Mer-
> ciful, who is helpful when one is in trouble. With prayer and fasting
> she commended all her anguish most urgently to Him. Meanwhile she
> had propounded to her secret self a ruse which presumed very far upon
> her Maker's courtesy. (p. 246)

The ruse is successful, and the episode concludes with Gottfried's
recognition that Christ is as accommodating to any who trust him as
a windblown sleeve.

> He falls into place and clings, whichever way you try Him, closely and
> smoothly, as He is bound to do. He is at the beck of every heart for
> honest deeds or fraud. Be it deadly earnest or game, He is just as you
> would have Him. (p. 248)

These extraordinary remarks, like the episode as a whole, have provoked a good deal of discussion. One doubts whether they are to be
taken as blasphemous or heretical, or as any more than a display of
rhetorical outrageousness that would have been expected to cause a
laugh as well as a ripple of excitement and apprehension and much
animated debate among Gottfried's listening audience. In any case,
legal ordeals, though not completely obsolete, were regarded by sophisticated churchmen as rather primitive, and mockery of the practice
might have been fashionably opportune.

The lovers are restored to favour and honour, or such honour as
can survive such manipulation of the truth. Soon Tristan goes away
on adventures, kills a giant, sends a little dog to Isolde, and returns to
court, where the lovers continue to make the best of stolen opportunities. But finally Mark banishes them, and they retire to the forest and
the 'Cave of Lovers', where they live in solitude and perfect bliss,
nourished, like the Desert Fathers, on love and desire. The cave is a
tabernacle in which the souls of the lovers come into communion on
the altar, cut from a slab of crystal, which is their bed. There can be
no doubt that in describing the grotto Gottfried is drawing deliberate
comparisons between the love of Tristan and Isolde and the rapt
eucharistic communion of the Christian mystic. It is not a serious
attempt to set up an 'alternative religion', nor is it merely a game, but
rather an extravagant display and codification and ritualization of the

emotions associated with sexual love. There is furthermore the daring suggestion that in noble hearts what was usually regarded as illicit love could be elevated to a high idealism, far from the sordid practicalities that surrounded marriage, and lofty in its obedience to the single imperative of dedication to love, for women as well as men – though all the time, of course, as we see in Gottfried's remarks about women, it was in the service of male libertinage. Gottfried concludes his diatribe against the instability and fickleness of women by reiterating that women are very subject to their appetites, but 'all honour and praise to the woman who nevertheless succeeds in abstaining! For when a woman grows in virtue despite her inherited instincts and gladly keeps her honour, reputation, and person intact, she is only a woman in name, but in spirit she is a man!' (pp. 277–8). The only compliment worth having, clearly.

Fearful that Mark will discover them while out hunting, Tristan devises a peephole for him, through which he sees the two of them in bed (on the stone altar) with a naked sword between them. Mark is something pleased with what he sees, and has them back to court, his motives irreparably mixed:

> He knew it as sure as death and saw full well that his wife Isolde was utterly absorbed in her passion for Tristan, heart and soul, yet he did not wish to know it. (p. 275)

But he keeps them under surveillance, and finally they are discovered, and, though Mark is still unwilling to act, Tristan declares they must part. He goes off to fight in Brittany, and wins the affection of another Isolde, whose name works upon him strangely. She reminds him of the first Isolde, which makes him sad, and so he cherishes the sight of her: 'The more Isolde broke his heart in Isolde's name, the more gladly he saw Isolde' (p. 291). He stays on, happily miserable yet increasingly attached.

Gottfried's poem breaks off here. The French of Thomas continues with the story of Tristan's wedding night and of how he remains true to the first Isolde by refraining from intercourse with his new bride, his motives explored in a long speech of introspection in the characteristically French manner. He returns to Cornwall, and then goes back to Brittany, where eventually he is wounded in battle with a poisoned spear and only Isolde of Cornwall can heal him (she must now fulfil the role earlier assigned to her mother). His friend Caerdin goes to fetch Isolde to heal him, his returning boat flying a white sail hoisted if Isolde comes with him. The boat is kept from landing by a storm and then by an unnatural calm. Isolde of Brittany (who we are told overheard the conversation of Tristan and Caerdin earlier) tells Tristan the sail is black (but it is implied that this might be because, in the extreme calm, all sails are hoisted) and he dies.

In *Tristan*, the lovers are freed from some of the customary obligations to virtuous behaviour by the special nature of the plot of the story, in which Love inflicts itself upon them through the magic love-potion. The apparent suspension of morality in the poem has this as its extenuation: Tristan and Isolde are overcome by a blind superior power, for which the potion itself serves as a metaphor. The potion relieves the lovers of guilt, and the narrative of the burden of attending to that guilt. This is how it comes to be that all the cheating and lying that follow (in which Mark is the only one who behaves honourably and generously) can be separated from questions of the goodness and badness of Tristan and Isolde as persons. The potion has placed them under the imperative of a higher power than their own will. Possibly, too, it could be said to act not merely as a magic cause of love but as a symbol of the passage from unconscious to conscious love. This is certainly how the imagined idea of a potion is used in a marvellous passage in Chaucer's *Troilus and Criseyde* (ii.649–51).

Tristan is one of the great poems of the Middle Ages, persistently subtle in its ironies, full of panache in its exercise of the skills of the romancer (the descriptions of jousting are both brilliantly vivid in themselves and also simultaneously a critique of the conventional rhetoric of such descriptions), and as penetrating as Chrétien or Chaucer in the analysis of the human heart (Isolde's 'secret self'). Gottfried's continual gossipy commentary on the action (like Chaucer's in *Troilus*) is an important aspect of the style of narration. Sometimes he will incorporate the audience in the commentary: pausing to comment on how Tristan is continually dogged by misfortune, he then inserts a protest from the reader, who thinks Tristan is doing well enough:

> Now in God's name, tell on! Tristan has just been knighted and achieved a brilliant success in matters of knightly honour – come tell us, what misfortune did he suffer with it? (p. 111)

A little later, he pulls himself up with fulsome apologies for having omitted a description of the Marshal Rual's wife Floraete:

> But what have I done? Oh where are my senses? I have made a blunder! To have passed over the Marshal's good wife, the faultless and constant Floraete – how unmannerly! (p. 113)

The apologies of course are insincere and draw attention with patrician dismissiveness to the appropriateness of neglecting such an unimportant little 'good wife'. Gottfried keeps up a constant barrage of comments and questions, as in the combat against Morold:

> Now some may well ask (and I myself ask it too): Where are God and Right now, Tristan's comrades-in-arms? Are they going to help him, I wonder? (p. 134)

This narrative intrusiveness, reminiscent of Chaucer and Fielding, but not of Henry James and the nineteenth-century novel of psychological realism, is part of the 'medieval/post-modern' texture of the poem, pushing the reader constantly out of participation and empathy and identification with the characters into a mixture of emotional involvement and alienated ironic detachment and scrutiny.

Tristan's fateful love for Isolde became the perfect vehicle for the French poet Thomas to explore the all-consuming surrender to sexual passion that was explicitly under indictment from clerical orthodoxy. Since the love of Tristan and Isolde was due to a magic potion, administered by mistake, they were liberated, in some sense, from the world of ordinary morality. In Gottfried's *Tristan*, the full outrageousness of a story based on such a proposition is exploited. The vein is often that of daring high comedy, and Gottfried's approach to the high idealized code of sexual love, with its rhetorical self-consciousness, bravura wit and pervasive irony, is very different from that of his contemporary Wolfram. Nevertheless, *Tristan* was for later artists the archetypal myth of sexual passion, passion that is dedicated to suffering, stimulated by obstruction (absence, marriage, social obligation, honour, loyalty to others), and satisfied only in death. Reinvigorated in German and English romanticism ('It is in death that love is sweetest, Death appears to one still alive as a nuptial night, the heart of sweet mysteries'),[7] this myth of passion and the intertwining of love and death found its climactic expression in Wagner's *Tristan und Isolde*.

4

Arthur, Lancelot and Gawain in Ricardian England

In the England of the late fourteenth century there are two Arthurian traditions. They exist side by side and are rewritten constantly as Arthurian romance continues to fulfil its role as the expression and embodiment of contemporary anxieties and aspirations about love, chivalry, heroism and society. The origins of the dual tradition have already been discussed in terms of transplantation – the way romance develops out of epic partly because of the way heroic stories migrate, lose their association with a national identity, and become vehicles for other kinds of socially significant statement.

The one tradition represents Arthur as a national hero, a battle-leader, a historical king, and narrates his rise to power, his flourishing, his conquests, and his fall and death. It is the native tradition, established as quasi-historical (though almost entirely fictitious) by Geoffrey of Monmouth, monumentally embodied in the great epic poem of the *Brut* by Layamon, dominant to a large extent in the romance-cum-epic of the alliterative *Morte Arthure*, and present still in Malory. Arthur is the centre of this body of narratives, Lancelot is either absent or has only a minor role quite unconnected with Guenevere, and the knights of the Round Table are part of Arthur's immediate retinue in his battle-exploits.

The other Arthurian tradition in England is the one that has come back into the country via France, having undergone the process of transmutation characteristic of transplantation. Arthur has lost his central role as a national hero, and has faded to a shadowy figure, an ineffectual *roi fainéant*, a mere husband, to accommodate the fashionable adulterous liaison of Lancelot and Guenevere. He is still the head of the order of the Round Table, but mostly Camelot is a place that individual knights go out from and come back to, and the king is there to wish them well when they leave and welcome them back when they return, or lament when they don't. The enormous influence of French literature in England during the thirteenth and fourteenth centuries, when the upper class was predominantly French-speaking, means that this was the tradition that was dominant.

First of all this dominance was exerted through romance in French, which remained the primary reading language of the upper classes of England right up until the time of Chaucer. If we look at lists of books owned by the aristocracy in the fourteenth century we find that they consist principally of books in French, and the exceptions are not English but Latin. Of those French books, most are Arthurian romances. By this time, though, Arthurian romance had become a little dated in France, the new fashion being for the love-allegories and love-visions derived from the *Roman de la Rose* that were being written by poets like Machaut, Froissart and Deschamps. English taste in French romance is increasingly provincial and old-fashioned, as Chaucer recognized.

The lack of attention to Arthurian material in Chaucer is in fact quite striking. He comments that his story of Chauntecleer and the fox in the Nun's Priest's Tale is as true as the story of Lancelot du Lake,

That wommen holde in ful greet reverence (*Canterbury Tales*, VII.3213);

he alludes to Gawain and his 'olde curtesye' in the Squire's Tale (*Canterbury Tales*, V.95); and to the days of King Arthur in the Wife of Bath's Tale, when all the land was 'fulfild of fayerye' (*Canterbury Tales*, III.859) – but is happily now filled only with friars. His attitude is patronizing, indulgent, maybe slightly sentimental, but certainly dismissive and even contemptuous, much like his attitude to traditional minstrel romance in the tale of Sir Thopas. It is the same with John Gower, Chaucer's contemporary: in the 130-odd exemplary tales that make up the bulk of Gower's 36,000-line *Confessio Amantis*, only one is taken from an Arthurian source, and that is the story of Tristram, only remotely Arthurian, which occupies eight lines in Book VI (467–75). Arthurian romance was clearly regarded at this time as an old-fashioned provincial taste, such as might characterize someone unsophisticated, 'up from the country'. The native heroic Arthurian tradition receives even less attention from these metropolitan poets. Does Chaucer ever think of England as a place where history was made or where his national loyalties might lie? I don't think so. He was a European poet who happened to write in English.

It was French Arthurian romance in French that was dominant among the upper classes in England up till the middle of the fourteenth century, but there was a second way in which this dominance was exerted, that is, through English adaptations of French Arthurian romances. These adaptations had been being made for some time, for an audience somewhat less court-centred or more provincial, a new and aspirant class of English readers, not well conversant with French but trying to come to grips with the cult of sophisticated love-sentiment in the French romances of their aristocratic superiors. A characteristic example is *Ywain and Gawain*, an abridgement of Chrétien's *Yvain* made in the mid-fourteenth century for a provincial audience, perhaps a minor baronial household. Though far from being a travesty of its original, and in many respects a careful professional adaptation for a different kind of audience, it shows little interest in Chrétien's subtle dialectic of love. Yvain's long debate with himself about the possibility of his love for the lady whose husband he has just slain being reciprocated occupies nearly eighty lines in Chrétien (1428–1506) but only ten in *Ywain and Gawain* (893–902). Ywain is much more manly, honest and truthful, much less abjectly submissive before his lady than he is in Chrétien, while the French poet's description of the lady's fashionably free flirtation with the knights of Arthur's retinue and his ridicule of those who are naive enough to take this sort of amorous attention as a sign of love (2454–65) is reduced to two lines as wholesome as porridge (1433–4). *Ywain and Gawain* was written at just the moment when French Arthurian romance had gone out of vogue. As English began to reoccupy the high ground as a language of literature, the ground from which it had been excluded by French and Anglo-Norman, the Arthurian romances that English translators and adapters found themselves working with had been superseded by the advent of the new love-poetry of Machaut and others, and were of no account in court and aristocratic circles. Yet to the English audiences of these newly translated French Arthurian romances, which we may take to be broadly speaking the aspirant urban bourgeoisie and the provincial gentry, and not the more exclusive circles of aristocratic and royal households, these poems may well have seemed the latest thing in romance, and a suitably glamorized version of the life of their social superiors.

There were thus two kinds of transplantation, one regional and the other social, and these two kinds of transplantation were both going on over a long period of time. It makes for a complex situation, but it is worth drawing attention to, if only to be reminded that we are still principally dealing with poems intended originally for oral delivery to a listening audience, with all the stylistic characteristics of such poetry. The poems may of course have been privately read on occasions, but there is no point in reading them as if they were intended for private reading – there is no point, to put it bluntly, in reading them slowly. Briskness is the essence of their narrative mode: the openness and diffuseness of their stylistic texture means that they will look threadbare, like a tapestry, if inspected too closely. Close reading of the kind that is so richly rewarding with Chaucer, or the *Gawain*-poet, or even the alliterative *Morte Arthure*, does not work well with the majority of these poems, which achieve their effects with broad strokes, over long stretches, and through the use of formulaic and conventional techniques rather than through any attempt at originality.

The alliterative *Morte Arthure* and the stanzaic *Morte Arthur* both deal with the last days of the Round Table and the death of Arthur, but they could hardly be more different. The former is heroic, martial, almost entirely preoccupied with warfare, and women play a part in it only as wives and potential mothers of dynasties (notice how Mordred marries Guenevere as a way of securing his claim to the throne) or as victims of lustful giants; Lancelot is there, but he is not the Lancelot we are used to. The stanzaic poem, by contrast, has the story that is more familiar to the modern reader from Malory and Tennyson, of the Round Table falling into disarray as a result of the conflict introduced by the adulterous liaison of Lancelot and Guenevere. It is about the conflict of passion and duty, of private and public responsibilities; women are important; fighting is less important. The presence in the same part of England, written at about the same time (*c.*1400), presumably by the same kind of poet for the same kind of audience, of two poems so completely different is an apt demonstration of the coexistence in England of the two principal traditions of the Arthurian story, the 'English' and the 'French'.

The Alliterative *Morte Arthure*

At the Christmas feast at Caerleon King Arthur receives the ambassadors of the Roman emperor Lucius demanding tribute and submission. He entertains them royally, but sends them back with denial and defiance. The council of his knights supports his stand and vow to do deeds of individual prowess in the war that must follow. Arthur gathers his army, makes Mordred viceroy, and sets sail. He has a dream of a dragon (himself) who kills a bear (the emperor). In Brittany, in single combat, he overcomes the giant of Mont-Saint-Michel and avenges the duchess of Brittany. After Gawain's embassy to Lucius and the running fight that follows, and after the ambush of Sir Cador in the forest, there follows the great battle of Augusta, in which Lucius is killed and his body sent in 'tribute' to Rome. There follows more fighting: the siege of Metz, Gawain's fight with Priamus, and the defeat of the imperial army in Lorraine. Arthur crosses the Alps into Italy and receives the surrender of the Romans at Viterbo. He determines to march on Rome but has a second dream, of Fortune's Wheel and the fall of the Nine Worthy, including himself. Immediately afterwards Cradok arrives with news of Mordred's seizure of power and marriage to Guenevere. Arthur returns to England and defeats Mordred in a sea-battle off the coast, but in the landing that follows Gawain, Arthur's greatest knight, is killed. Mordred returns to Cornwall; Arthur grieves and vows vengeance. In the last battle Mordred is killed but also mortally wounds Arthur, who grieves over his dead knights, dies and is buried in Glastonbury.

The poem is written in alliterative verse, that is, unrhymed four-stress lines with alliteration on stressed syllables as the structural bonding of the line, and the form needs to be talked about, since there is no doubt that it is intended to draw attention to itself. Sometimes it seems to be all poetry and no sense, as if the poet were in a fever of intoxication. The diction, imagery and syntax all bear witness to a pursuit of the striking and extravagant, a kind of controlled abandon, for instance in the use of alliteration on consecutive lines (something which is very rare elsewhere in alliterative poetry), often with difficult consonant-groups, as if to demonstrate a virtuoso-like power:

> Swiftly with swordes   they swappen thereafter,
> Swappes down full sweperly · sweltande knightes;

So many sways in swogh,   swoonand at ones,
That all sweltes on swarth   that they over-swingen.

(464–7)

[swappen, 'strike'; sweperly, 'swiftly'; sweltande, 'dying'; in swogh, 'in a faint'; swarth, 'ground'; over-swingen, 'cut down']

At lines 2755–65, in a *tour de force* of alliterative bravado, no fewer than eleven successive lines alliterate on f. Of course, knights tend to be manufactured for the purpose with names beginning with f- (Florent or Floridas or Feraunt), rather than having to be fitted into the verse because their names begin with f-, and of course they have to come from places like Famagusta and Friesland. But there is no sense of constraint – it is almost as if the poet is revelling in his verbal invention and daring.

There is delight, ingenuity and self-regard in the rhetorical poetic of the alliterative *Morte Arthure*, and a self-conscious 'poeticness' which modern readers, looking for a telling of the story that values speed and economy and encourages sympathetic identification with the actors, may find intrusive. But it is only an extreme form of the conscious 'textuality' that characterizes medieval poetry, the force with which its rhetoric holds the reader at a distance, as in Chrétien and Gottfried. It is a distance worth working for.

But the poem is also a pondered retelling of the story, and one that takes the story seriously, much more like epic than romance. There are many references to chivalry and knighthood and to Arthur as the exemplar of chivalry, but essentially Arthur is a warrior-king, the leader of the nation, the king in whom the nation is embodied; the sentiments are almost purely heroic, with emphasis throughout on war and battle not as a means of self-testing and self-proving more or less gratuitously engaged in, but as the business of territorial defence and aggression. The close association of Arthur with his principal knights, especially Gawain, reminds one of the Germanic *comitatus* or of the relationship of Charlemagne and Roland. The love-interest is almost totally absent, and Guenevere is given a totally non-romantic role as an instrument of Mordred's ambition; there is no suggestion that she has fallen in love with Mordred – the very idea is ridiculous.

Arthur is a public figure, the embodiment of the nation, and everything he does is resonant with public implication, but his motives and actions remain those of a man put in that position, not of some allegorical or idealized personage. It is a long way from romance, where the adventures and ordeals that the hero is put to are those that any knight might be put to, enactments of processes of suffering and learning that are appropriate to the whole class. What Arthur experiences has no generalizable meaning; it is what happened in history, once, uniquely; no one else will have to face Arthur's problems. The poem is essentially an exploration of the meaning of history, and of the relation of one man's actions and motives to events that he purports to have power over (he is king, after all), but hardly seems to be in control of. The man-as-king is 'condemned' to historical action – Arthur, in this poem, could not just have become a penitent, or undergone some fantasy cryogenic transmigration to Avalon.

The concentration is on Arthur – the story is of his kingship in triumph and fall. The two dreams are strategically placed to chart the development of the story. Dreams in medieval narrative function in various ways, as omens and premonitions and warnings and plot-devices, but they always involve some commentary on the action from a position beyond the understanding of the persons who dream them, coming as they do from beyond their intentionality. The first dream, of the dragon and the bear, is like a supernatural endorsement of Arthur's kingship and of his aggressive defence of the nation's pride against the insolence of foreigners. It would have been appropriate at the time of the French wars of Edward III or Henry V, and indeed at almost any time when England was involved in continental wars – so much so that it would be rash to look for anything too specific in the way of topical reference. Everything that Arthur has done up to the time of the dream has been superbly kingly: the measured courtesy with which he treated the Roman ambassadors, the iron control that he exerted over his own anger and over the outrage of his followers, the lavishness of his entertainment for the ambassadors, the care that he takes to consult his council of knights, and the lofty contempt with which he gives his answer combined with scrupulous concern for the safe-conduct of the ambassadors to the Channel port of Sandwich. Arthur's subsequent arrangements for the care of the kingdom during his absence show a very proper sense of responsibility (it is a nice touch of irony that shows Mordred reluctant to take on the job of viceroy), and the dream of the dragon and the bear leads into the fight against the giant of Mont-Saint-Michel, which shows Arthur at the height of his kingly powers – as a warrior and as a defender of his people. Some have seen his declaration that he will take on the fight alone – 'For I will seek this saint by myselve one' (937) – as a sign of vaingloriousness, but it is more the traditional boldness of the great warrior, like Roland refusing to blow his horn till the last (and too late) moment, or Beowulf entering the dragon's lair alone, leaving his twelve companions outside. And the giant after all is genuinely wicked, about as wicked as even a giant could be, eating children and raping women, and killing him is almost a Christ-like act.

The second dream is the dream of Fortune's Wheel, in which Arthur learns of the mutability of Fortune and how even the greatest warrior and king is in the end brought low. The philosopher who explains the dream to him takes the opportunity to add a little moralizing –

> 'Thou hast shed much blood, and shalkes destroyed,
> Sakeles, in surquidrie, in sere kinges landes'
> (3398–9) –

[shalkes, 'men'; Sakeles, 'innocent'; surquidrie, 'pride'; sere, 'many']

and this comment has commonly been used in the attempt to locate the tragedy of Arthur in the defect in his nature of overweening pride and imperialistic ambition. It has been pointed out that there was an accepted definition of the 'just war' in medieval chivalric manuals: that wars for justice, against oppression and usurpation, are lawful, while wars for revenge or aggression are unlawful. It has been argued that Arthur's wars up to the siege of Metz are righteous wars, but when he sets his sights on Rome, or even on world dominion – 'We shall be overling of all that on erthe lenges' (3211) – he engages in wars of aggression and is doomed to fall. An apparent shift has been detected in Arthur's attitude to fighting. Early on, he does what needs to be done, and no more: he rebukes Cador, who has just fought his way out of a Roman ambush, for taking such risks as have led to the loss of many good knights (1920–7). But later in the story, at the siege of Metz, when Gawain engages in just such a rash adventure in going out quite gratuitously (like a romance-hero) to look for someone to fight, Arthur congratulates him.

There is much that is persuasive in these views,[1] especially in their attempt to make of the poem something more than the usual medieval tragedy of Fortune, with its monotonous catalogue, as in Chaucer's Monk's Tale, of those who have fallen from prosperity into adversity.

Whether the argument of the just war holds it is hard to say: it was an academic concept, and in any case the conquest of Rome had always been the game-plan; it is not a new idea. Moreover, the war is represented as a crusade against evil, with Saracens and giants and other monstrous beings fighting on the enemy side. The reproof of the philosopher who interprets the dream is a warning to Arthur that he will die and should repent of all his killing, but it was recognized that all who killed even in a just war had to do penance (as Shakespeare's Henry V explains to the soldiers on the night before Agincourt). Arthur is criticized for being a warrior rather than for being a wanton aggressor. The poem has no easy answer to the opposed demands of the heroic and the piously moral.

One could see, as Lee Patterson does, in an important essay, a deep flaw within the poem, an unresolved inner conflict, and trace it back as he does to the inception of the Arthur story.[2] Conceived by Geoffrey of Monmouth as a Virgilian narrative of secular history, a means through which the political legitimacy of England's Norman rulers could be asserted in terms of cyclic invasion and conquest, it was from the start riddled with doubts – both suspicion as to its authenticity, and a dark side both to Arthur's birth (deceit, near-adultery, the death of his mother's husband) and to his death, at the hands of the son born of an apparently incestuous union with his half-sister. It is 'a myth of origins that deconstructs the origin' (Patterson, p. 202), and was transmitted to its successors carrying this virus of instability. The only certainty therefore in the story is not heroism or some other transcendent princely virtue but the iron law of recurrence – the Wheel of Fortune. The attempt is to find a legitimation of the political present in the past, but all that can be found is recursion to disaster. 'The present is not a fulfilment of the past but a re-enactment' (p. 224). All there is a place for at the end is penitence and the heroism of a good death, and on our part pity for the kings who have to go through the motions of choice and action while bound to the Wheel. 'The pathos of monarchy solicits our political consent' (p. 230). This is certainly true to the experience of the poignant ending of the poem, but leaves something unsaid about the grandeur of Arthur's doomed heroism.

One might therefore want to reach back into the experience of the poem, from Patterson's bleak and powerful analysis of its significance, to find again in the portrayal of Arthur a tragic quality, especially in his acceptance of the inevitability of suffering. One of the great strengths of the poem is that Arthur seems to grow into an awareness of the dilemma of the king and the man, not as a response to the speech of the philosopher but through the death of Gawain and the intolerable recognition it brings of mortality. Gawain's action in wading ashore with his small band and taking on the whole enemy army is condemned over and over again as rash and foolhardy (3802, 3817, 3826, 3836), yet it is the epitome of the heroic spirit and calls forth a noble tribute from Mordred (3874–85), who turns from the battle lamenting that it was ever his fate to be the instrument of such destruction:

> Went weepand away   and weryes the stounde
> That ever his werdes wer wrought   such wandreth to work.
> > (3888–9)

[weryes, 'curses'; stounde, 'time'; werdes, 'fate'; wandreth, 'trouble']

When Arthur comes upon Gawain's body, his grief is uncontrollable, and he is reproached for it by his knights:

> 'Be knightly of countenaunce als a king sholde,
> And leve such clamour, for Cristes love of heven!'
> > (3979–80)

But it is not in the nature of the heroic spirit to be sensible and reasonable, and Arthur not only tries to gather Gawain's blood in his hands and put it in a helmet – in direct allusion to the eucharistic chalice – but in an unexpected turn he takes upon himself all the sinfulness of Gawain. Gawain is 'sakless [innocent] of sin' (3992) – 'He is sakless surprised for sin of mine one [alone]' (3986). This can only refer to Arthur's general bellicoseness, since it was repeatedly stated that Gawain's stepping ashore was a wild and foolish act, but I think we should associate it with a general magnanimity on Arthur's part, as he takes upon himself all the burden of guilt and suffering which Shakespeare's Henry V so positively declared to be the responsibility of the individual soldier.

So too when he sees the destruction of his knights in the last battle:

> 'Why then ne had Drighten   destained at his dere will
> That He had deemed me today to die for you all?'
> > (4157–8)

It is again as if he sees a role for the king not just as one who lives and fights for his people but as one who dies for them too, dies that they may live. As the battlefield in himself of the conflict between the heroic energy of living and the tragic recognition of the necessity of death, Arthur is much more than the victim of an exemplary moral narrative, much more a tragic figure in himself. The essence of that conflict is in his final speeches, the first lamenting the loss of all his knights of the Round Table, with the extraordinary image of himself as a widow bewailing the loss of her child:

> 'I may helpless on hethe house by mine one
> Als a woeful widow that wantes her berne'
>   (4284–5);

the second thanking God for all the glories he has granted and for victory in this last battle (4296–4300). At the end he gives his final commands for the disposal of his remains and the succession to the kingdom, and performs his last kingly duty in an act in which the horror and cruelty of historical necessity are set starkly against the glory and magnanimity of the heroic life:

> 'And sithen merk manly to Mordred's children,
> That they be slely slain and slongen in waters;
> Let no wicked weed wax ne writhe on this erthe . . .
> If Waynor have wel wrought, well her betide!'
>   (4320–6)

[merk, 'go'; slely, 'prudently'; writhe, 'flourish']

There is a bitter reminder here that Guenevere bore no children to Arthur, and that the lack of a legitimate heir was a contributory factor in his downfall.

The Stanzaic *Morte Arthur*

Where the alliterative *Morte Arthure* goes back to Geoffrey of Monmouth and the 'English' tradition of Arthur, the stanzaic poem of *Le Morte Arthur* is derived from a version of the French *Mort Artu*, part of the

great Vulgate cycle of Arthurian romance, and thus centrally representative of the 'French' Arthurian tradition. It is the finest English
poem in this tradition: it takes up the story of the love-affair of
Lancelot and Guenevere at the moment when it is recognized to be
doomed, and treats it with tenderness and pathos and a melancholy
sense of inevitability.

An important difference between the alliterative and stanzaic
poems and the two traditions they represent is in the nature of their
endings. There are no pious consolations at the end of the alliterative
Morte Arthure – even the isle of Avalon is treated as a name for the
real place of Glastonbury, where Arthur is really buried. But at the
end of the stanzaic *Morte Arthur*, the monasteries take over: Arthur is
buried in one, Guenevere goes into a nunnery, and Lancelot spends
the last years of his life in an odour of sanctity, his former warrior-
followers acting as acolytes. Familiar pieties displace the tragic contemplation of the unique realities of existence, and we are reminded
of the essential incompatibility of tragedy and the Christian faith. All
the insight that tragedy gives into the capacity of human beings to
suffer and to learn, to triumph whether inwardly or outwardly over
the brute force of circumstance, to constitute themselves as an objec-
tion to the predicament of destiny, is blurred if the tragic hero is seen
to be accepting a postdated cheque on the hereafter. There are no
rewards for good behaviour in tragedy, only grim satisfaction on our
part at the demonstration of the power of human beings to be fully
human. Some of that quality of tragedy is present in the alliterative
Morte Arthure; in the stanzaic *Morte Arthur* the impact of the tragedy is
softened into pathos, and deflected into piety. The reason is not far to
seek: the Vulgate cycle was compiled under the influence of monastic
spirituality, the primary concern of which was to demonstrate that
the secular chivalry of Arthur was nothing beside the spiritual chivalry of the religious life, and to show above all how the failure of the
Round Table was written into its failure in the Grail. In the *Mort Artu*,
which is part of the Vulgate cycle and the source of the stanzaic *Morte
Arthur*, the Round Table is already doomed, and an atmosphere of
foreboding hangs over everything. The only recourse when everything falls apart is to turn to the religious life, which everyone who is
left alive does at the end.

The poem falls into six sections: (1) Lancelot goes incognito to the
tournament at Winchester, wearing the favour of the maid of Astolat.

He is badly wounded and returns to Astolat, where he is found by Gawain, who reports to the queen that the maid has become Lancelot's mistress (which is not true). She is distressed and reproaches Lancelot when he returns, and he retires to the wilderness much mortified. (2) Mador accuses the queen of trying to kill a knight of the Round Table with a poisoned apple. Meanwhile the body of the maid of Astolat comes floating down the river with a letter that makes it clear she was not Lancelot's mistress. Guenevere is very angry with Gawain. Lancelot returns in disguise to be her champion against Mador. (3) Agravain and his friends plot to trap Lancelot and Guenevere. The plot fails but Guenevere is condemned nevertheless to be burnt as an adulteress. Lancelot in rescuing her accidentally kills Gaheriet, Gawain's brother, which earns him the undying enmity of Gawain. He retires to Joyous Gard in France, where he is besieged by Arthur and Gawain. (4) The pope intervenes to make peace. Guenevere is returned to Arthur, but Gawain refuses to be reconciled, and Arthur and Gawain again invade France. Lancelot's offer of peace is refused; he keeps defeating Gawain in battle but is reluctant to kill him. (5) News comes of Mordred's treachery. Arthur returns, Gawain is killed, and the last battle is fought, despite an attempt by Arthur, warned by Gawain in a dream that Lancelot is coming to help, to have it postponed. Arthur is mortally wounded and carried off to Avalon after the episode with Bedivere and the casting of the sword into the lake. (6) Lancelot returns to find Arthur dead and Guenevere in a nunnery. He retires to a monastery himself, where he dies. Guenevere dies too.

The stanzaic *Morte Arthur* is written in an alternate-rhyming eight-line stanza, with a limited, repetitious and stylized diction and a simple syntax. The formalization and ritualization of the style, which acts of course to formalize and ritualize the narrative and disengage us from its reality, is very marked, for instance in the use of stanzaic repetition, where similar events will be reported in the same words. Battle-descriptions are often done in this way (2102, 2150, 2464, 2524). This kind of incremental repetition, or repetition with variation, is very characteristic of traditional oral poetry, particularly the ballad, and the stanzaic *Morte Arthur* has much in common with the cryptic, laconic, gesture-like style of such poetry. It may strike us as thin and diffuse, accustomed as we are to the loading of every rift with ore that private reading makes possible, but the context of the listening audience needs to be recreated or imagined, and also the receptiveness of that audience to the evocativeness of such ritualized language. Repetition with variation is particularly effective in speech exchanges in ritualizing and ceremonializing the expression of powerful feeling. There is a beautiful example in Guenevere's repeated solicitations to the knights of the court to act as her champion against Mador (1324–1403), and another in Lancelot's warnings to Arthur to leave off the war (2842–9, 2930–7). Another form of repetition called concatenation ('chaining'), where the first line of a stanza repeats in varied form the last line of the preceding stanza, helps to create an almost overwhelming poignancy, as in the scene between Lancelot and Guenevere at the end (3662–3713). Malory is often praised for his handling of this scene, but all the essential elements are already present in the stanzaic *Morte Arthur*, his source at this point, including the outrageous yet endearing sentimentality of contriving such a scene at all, and the pert piety of Guenevere's reply to the request for a kiss:

> 'Madame', then said Launcelot du Lake,
> 'Kiss me, and I shall wend as-tite.'
> 'Nay,' said the queen, 'that will I not;
> Launcelot, think on that no more;
> To abstain us we moste have thought
> Fro such we have delited in ere.
> Let us think on Him That us hath bought,
> And we shall plese God therefore.
> Think on this world, how there is nought
> But war and strife and batail sore.'
>   (3712–21)

[wend as-tite, 'go quickly away'; moste, 'must'; ere, 'before']

The story that is told in this stylized manner is largely allowed to tell itself. The 'author' could hardly be more absent. Dialogue becomes particularly important, and the handling of it is very expressive, perhaps through the very restraint of the exchanges, especially between Lancelot and Guenevere (for example, 69–80, 736–75). The simplicity of the language in their conversations speaks volumes of what lies at the heart, as a form of gesture rather than self-expression, where the outward releases the inward through a subtle series of conventional signals. It is formalized, stylized, hackneyed even, yet strangely evocative. The lovers do not in fact really have conversations: they speak in the coded language of courtesy, and never explain anything to each other or think about ways of avoiding catastrophe. They are frozen into the ritual tableaux of inaction that give such pathetic inevitability to the story. The formalized, stylized quality of the verse matches that of the characters.

Guenevere throughout has a melancholy and decorous resignation. Her whole life is weeping, as if she were aware that she had a part in a long threnody upon the dream of Camelot. Lamentation for what is past is her reaction to impending disaster, as the twelve knights led by Agravain clamour at the chamber-door:

> 'Wele-away,' then said the queen,
> 'Launcelot, what shal worthe of us two?
> The love that hath been us between,
> To such ending that it sholde go!'
>
> (1816–19)

[worthe, 'become']

But the epitome of this courtesy, this restraint and decorum, this dignified suppression of all base feeling, all appetite of self and survival, is Lancelot. We see it in the flawless politeness yet honesty of his reply to the maid of Astolat:

> 'Lady,' he said, 'thou moste let;
> For me ne gif thee nothing ill;
> In another stede mine herte is set;
> It is not at mine owne wille'
>
> (201–4);

[moste let, 'must stop'; gif thee, 'make yourself'; stede, 'place']

and in the forbearance which makes him stay his hand from killing Arthur and Gawain (2142–5) and set Arthur on his horse again after he has been knocked off it by Bors (2190–3). The note of elegy is sounded again:

> When the king was horsed there,
> Launcelot lookes he upon,

How courtaisy was in him more
Than ever was in any man.
He thought on thinges that had been ere;
The teres from his eyen ran;
He said, 'Alas,' with sighing sore,
'That ever yet this war began!'

(2198–2205)

All this moving detail we shall see again in Malory, but hardly more evocatively treated than here.

There is much that one could find missing in the stanzaic *Morte Arthur*: the characters are stylized, the conflict at the heart of the narrative is only imperfectly realized, there is a certain monotony in the prevailing mood of twilight melancholy. But for those who wish to hear the authentic note of romance, 'the indescribable plaintive melody, the sigh of the wind over the enchanted ground', here it is.[3]

Sir Gawain and the Green Knight

Sir Gawain and the Green Knight was written towards the end of the fourteenth century by an unknown poet. Whether or not he was also the poet of *Pearl, Cleanness* and *Patience* (all in the same unique manuscript), he is one of the greatest poets of the English language. He writes in alliterative verse, with the long lines divided into stanzas of irregular length by means of the short rhymed lines of the 'bob-and-wheel', which are subtly a form of narrative punctuation, recapitulation, anticipation or ironic commentary. Alliterative verse was associated with the north-west of England rather than with London, but there is no provinciality here in the understanding of courtly culture or the conventions of romance. The only provinciality is in the dialect, which is difficult, and made even more so by the poet's energy in lexical innovation and experimentation.

The poem opens by reminding us briefly of the legendary history of Britain and the Trojan ancestry of Arthur, and passes to a description of the Christmas feast at Arthur's court, full of youth and joy, and in its 'first age' (line 54), before the shadow of the Grail has fallen upon it, or the adulterous liaison of Lancelot and Guenevere. New Year's

Day arrives, and a gigantic green knight rides into the hall and throws down a challenge: that someone in the company cut off his head now with a huge axe that he carries and then come in a year's time to the Green Chapel and submit to the same fate. Arthur himself, spurred by the Green Knight's insolence, seizes the axe, but Gawain, in a speech of impeccable politeness, persuades him that it would be more appropriate for a less important person to take up a 'game' that seems rather silly (what likelihood is there of a second round?). Gawain decapitates the Green Knight at a single blow, whereupon the Knight picks up his head and, after reminding Gawain of his promise, gallops out of the hall. The poem is divided into 'fits' (successive portions of narrative that might be recited or read out at a sitting) and the first fit ends here.

The year passes, Gawain departs for the unknown Green Chapel, and travels in bitter winter cold through hostile mountain landscape until on Christmas morning he comes upon the castle of Hautdesert. He is warmly welcomed by the lord Bercilak and urged to stay over until New Year's Day, when Bercilak will direct him to the Green Chapel, which is nearby. After the Christmas festivities, during which Gawain meets Bercilak's beautiful wife and her ugly old female companion, the lord suggests a game: he will go out each day hunting, Gawain will stay at home and be entertained by the lady of the house, and at the end of each day they will exchange winnings.

The third fit, an elaborate triple triptych-like structure, follows the events of the next three days. Each day the lord goes hunting (in turn the deer, the boar and the fox) and in the midst of the hunt the narration switches to Gawain's bedroom, where the lady attempts with some skill and determination to seduce him, after which the narrative of the hunt is resumed and completed. It is a not uncommon situation for the Gawain of the French tradition, nor is his resistance usually prolonged, but Gawain in this English poem is not only courteous but also faithful in his allegiance to the Virgin Mary and in his observance of the virtues symbolized in the pentangle that he carries blazoned on his shield. He faithfully pays to the lord the kiss that he wins on the first day and the two kisses that he wins on the second day, and receives in return the trophies of the day's hunting. On the third day, having seemingly given up her attempts at seduction, the lady presses him to accept a love-gift of a ring. When he refuses, she offers him instead a simple green girdle (a belt, or sash) which has the magic power of protecting its wearer from any harmful blow. In a moment of weakness, Gawain accepts it, promising to conceal it from the lord. At the evening's exchange of winnings he gives him three kisses instead.

Next morning Gawain sets off with a guide, through another marvellously realized winter landscape, for the Green Chapel. He arrives there alone: it is nothing but an old cave. Confronted by the fearsome Green Knight, he submits his head to the axe, at first with understandable apprehension but then, exasperated by the Green Knight's taunts and repeated feinted blows, with fierce determination. At the third stroke, the Green Knight cuts him with a little nick in the neck and then, when Gawain springs back in joyous relief at having survived the encounter, reveals himself as no other than Bercilak, changed into this shape by the magic of Morgan le Fay, the old woman at the castle, in order to test the mettle of the Round Table. Gawain has performed well, he declares, his only fault being the breaking of his promise on the third day, for which he received the nick in the neck at the third stroke. Gawain is mortified, angry and humiliated, and refuses all commendation of his near-success. He returns to court wearing the girdle as the symbol of his shame. Arthur and the court welcome him back, try to laugh him out of his discomfiture, and agree that all shall wear the girdle as a badge of honour.

Gawain, it seems, has been trapped in an impossible situation, in an infernal narrative machine designed to demonstrate the contradictions at the heart of the chivalric code. Should he seek at all costs to preserve his promise to the lord, or his chastity, or the single-minded devotion to the Virgin blazoned on his shield, or his reputation for courtesy, or his life? He does his best, and he doesn't do badly, but 'not doing badly' is not enough for a knight of romance and he ends the poem humiliated and angry. The story is cunningly designed so as to put to the test the compromises that had long maintained chivalric love-romance in its precious and uneasy equilibrium. Also, Gawain is now in a world in which the traditional questions asked of a questing knight are put in terms of a materialized world of real feelings and fears, real internal conflicts, real landscapes. The winter landscape through which Gawain rides on his quest, the rough rock-strewn hill-terrain of the hunts, the snow-covered and mist-capped hills of the last journey to the Green Chapel, are not part of Gawain's quest for self-realization and knightly identity: they are really there.

Sir Gawain and the Green Knight is thus a romance transplanted into a new dimension of the real. The poem takes as its hero a well-known figure of French romance with two main attributes – a reputation for courtesy, and a habit of getting into awkward and embarrassing situations with women – and puts him into a new kind of story in which the usual rules do not pertain, and in which public honour and private virtue, the public self and the private self, become inextricably entangled. In one sense, it is a comedy-romance. Gawain plays his part in a game in which the rules have been changed without his knowing it (one of the basic comic structures – though neither do we at first) so that the result of the first test depends on success in the second, and it's not entirely clear what success in the second would consist of.

This sense that the story is not fair to its protagonist or to us is an unusual and invigorating experience – suggestive of a story with autonomous meaning, not subject to authorial predication – and piquancy is added by hints of other knotty problems in the plot which may have deeper meanings (or which may be red herrings). The offer of the magic girdle (quite specifically not as a love-token) offers a lifeline out of the danger that Gawain, with all his other delicate problems of conduct, must always have been most conscious of. But is he entitled to take it? Yes, because romance-heroes are always accepting talismans of this kind to protect them from danger. No, because if he takes it, intending to make use of it, he will have to keep it and therefore not give it back to Bercilak under the exchange of winnings agreement. But surely he has an obligation to try to save his life, especially since the Green Knight 'cheated' by picking up his head after it had been chopped off; anyway, wasn't the exchange of winnings agreement just a game? It is an impossible conundrum, and nothing is solved by Gawain's confession to the priest immediately after accepting the girdle. Some critics take this to be a false confession and therefore a proof of felonious intent. Gawain is not only cheating his host but trying to cheat God. But the priest, we are told, confesses Gawain as clean as the day he was born. One wonders, indeed, what any priest in his senses might have made of a 'confession' about a game of exchanges and a magic girdle.

There is also the tantalizing suggestiveness of the scene in which Gawain's guide on his journey to the Green Chapel warns him of the danger he is in and promises not to let anyone know if Gawain simply sneaks off home. Gawain will have nothing to do with this and expresses a brave, stoical determination to face up to his fate, as we should expect. But what if his courage derives from the girdle he is wearing (we are told in detail about his care to put it on that morning)? In that case, his behaviour would appear slimily hypocritical. And what if it really is the girdle that saves his life? He receives a nick in the neck on the third stroke, because he slipped slightly in accepting the girdle, with the implication that if he hadn't accepted it he would have got off scot-free; but the implication may equally well be that without the girdle he would have had his head chopped off.

At the end, there are more questions. The court laughs, pleased to see Gawain back, and playfully determines to share the badge of his dishonour as a sign of honour. This may be understood as a form of social reintegration – life must go on. Is Gawain's persistence in self-accusation and self-mortification –

> 'For none may hyden his harme bot unhap ne may hitte,
> For there hit ones is tached twynne wil hit never'
>
> (2511–12) –

[unhap, 'misfortune'; hitte, 'strike'; tached, 'attached'; twynne, 'be separated']

– a sign of pride and refusal to recognize the inevitability of human imperfection? Or does he not understand, despite his use of the formulae of Christian confession, the provision of Christian forgiveness? Or is he the only one who truly understands what he is really guilty of? The idea that the story is a machine infallibly designed to trap him and then to release him, with laughter, is not far from our minds, but yet not quite enough.

Questions like this make the reading and discussing of the poem a perennially fascinating activity. Many of the questions arise because of the unexpected insights we are given into Gawain's interior consciousness, as for instance into the dilemma he faces with the lady:

> He cared for his cortaysye, lest crathayn he were,
> And more for his meschef if he schulde make synne
> And be traytor to that tulk that that telde aghte.
>
> (1773–5)

[crathayn, 'a churl'; meschef, 'harm'; tulk, 'knight'; telde, 'house'; aghte, 'owned']

It is in the 'showdown' scene, when he finds out that what he has done was already being talked about, and indeed was planned in advance, that Gawain drops into the abyss of the interior self. It is not what he did that so fills him with embarrassment, but that he was found out in the way that he was; as Burrow says, 'Only when he is actually dishonoured by the censure of a fellow knight does he feel its shame'.[4] He was apparently quite happy with his chosen course of action until then, or rather he was content to act as if he did not realize what he was doing: 'as for many chivalric heroes', says Spearing,[5] 'the criteria of conduct are not fully internalized'. Once he had accepted the girdle, he behaved with the noble courtesy and courage that was customary to his public self and that constructed also his private self. Now he is aware of the gap between the two that existed all the time, of the lies that he has told to himself, of the disunity of his personality; he is 'ashamed of himself'.

To show a fictional character capable of being embarrassed and humiliated in the way that Gawain is embarrassed and humiliated is a new art of the interior self (though not, one presumes, a new experience for human beings) that is being disentangled from the fictions of chivalry that had prevailed. Yvain, faced with the shame and humiliation of having forgotten his promise to Laudine, in Chrétien's *Yvain*, can only run mad in the woods. Lancelot behaves similarly when accused by Guenevere of disloyalty. This is the customary response to extreme embarrassment in medieval romance: it constitutes a kind of mental suicide, a revulsion against the pain inflicted on the inner self so violent that mental life must be suspended, blocked off, until some form of redemption becomes available. Gawain goes through all the painful stages of self-recognition when he finds that he has been the unwitting subject of a kind of research experiment to determine whether the 'surquidre' of the Round Table (2457) is all that it is renowned to be. He feels anger, irritation, dismay, shame, self-loathing, and it is no comfort to him that the experiment is said to have been largely positive in its results, and that he is thought to have done fairly well (2364–8). But Gawain does not go mad, or run wild in the woods. He shows a capacity for bearing his shame and turning it into the story of his life that puts him with the Ancient Mariner rather than with Yvain or Lancelot or Tristram. Dead to honour, he must live by a thousand self-narrations. A possible distinction can be made here between the public nature of 'shame', as part of a system of values, able to be expiated, exploited or revenged, and the private nature of 'embarrassment', which is an inseparable part of one's private being.[6] For Gawain, in his newly discovered solitariness, there is nothing to be done, no action that will cleanse and renew his humiliated self, no person, however well disposed, who will properly understand what has happened to him, but the quality he has found in himself is the quality in individuals that we have become accustomed to believe constitutes them in their essential individual humanity.

Sir Gawain and the Green Knight is not only a witty and absorbing exploration of the boundaries of the inner self and the outer self; it is also a great poem, in the sense that the drama of the action and its impact on the senses and feelings of the characters is registered in the verse with consistent richness, depth and vigour. The poet's use of external gesture to convey inward feeling, for instance, is remarkably vivid. Scornful of the silence with which his challenge has been greeted, the Green Knight turns abruptly in his saddle, rolls his red eyes menacingly around, bends his bristling brows in a frown, throws up his head so that his beard sticks out, and clears his throat noisily (303–8) before beginning his sardonic taunting speech. A little later, the horror of the court as the Green Knight's decapitated head rolls towards them is almost palpable as they thrust at it nervously with their feet (428). Even the experience of the animals being hunted is made real for us.

But it is the effect of the action upon Gawain that we are made to feel most vividly and persistently. The year that passes as Gawain waits to set out on his journey to the Green Chapel is described in the evocative language of seasonal change –

> And thus yirnes the yere in yisterdayes mony,
> And wynter wyndes ayayn, as the world askes
> (529–30) –

[yirnes, 'passes'; wyndes ayayn, 'comes round again']

that suggests the mutability of human life and gives a poignant echo to what is most in Gawain's mind. Gawain's sensations, his bodily experience, are made real for us in a manner quite exceptional in medieval romance. On his journey north, we are told, it was not the giants and dragons and monsters that caused him most trouble but the more mundane discomforts of winter:

> Nere slayn with the slete he slepte in his yrnes
> Mo nightes then innogh in naked rokkes.
>
> (729–30)

[yrnes, 'irons' [armour]; Mo, 'more'; innogh, 'enough']

All the more luxuriant is the warmth of the reception at the castle – one of the most appealing passages in the poem – where we feel what it was like to be hospitably received after an arduous winter-journey, the warmth, the fresh clothing, the delicious snacks, the spiced drinks, and of course the women. It is no surprise when Gawain, flushed with wine after the privations of his journey, pursues the young châtelaine a little too eagerly into the chapel (935–6) and has to be restrained by the lord's hand on his sleeve. In a virtuoso passage, the movement of Gawain's hidden consciousness is tracked through the very sounds and syntax of the verse, as he 'decides' to accept the girdle. There is no self-consciously staged inner debate here, but a slithering of fear and desire into self-justification and willed but unself-aware act:

> Then cast the knight, and hit come to his hert
> Hit were a juel for the jopardy that hym jugged were
> When he acheved to the chapel his chek for to fech;
> Myght he have slypped to be vnslayn, the slyght were noble.
>
> (1855–8)

[cast, 'considered'; juel, 'jewel'; acheved to, 'reached'; chek, 'fortune'; fech, 'receive'; slyght, 'device']

The slipperiness of the planned escape from death is well conveyed in the consonants of 'slypped to be vnslayn', while the queasiness of the self-justification is present in the stubborn oxymoron of 'the slyght were noble'. We watch the fault-line open between Gawain's public self and his private self.

5

Malory's *Morte D'Arthur*

Sir Thomas Malory's *Morte D'Arthur* marks a new age in English writing – it is one of the earliest works to be brought out for the first time in a printed edition, that of Caxton in 1485 – but it is also a deliberate return to and recovery of the past. Malory goes back for his story to the French Vulgate cycle of over two centuries before and also incorporates material from the two English *Morte Arthur* poems of a century before. Malory shared with Caxton and others in the late fifteenth century an idealizing admiration for the golden age of chivalry (which of course had never existed except as an imagined goal for aspiration or an escape from reality), and a desire to find in Arthur and the Round Table the lineaments of a great and noble society. In the same year that the *Morte* was published, Henry VII seized the throne, claiming Arthurian ancestry for the new Tudor dynasty and in the following year naming his first-born son Arthur.

If Malory was seeking a way of expressing a renewed idealism about chivalry – perhaps as a reaction to his own experience of the sordid realities of the Wars of the Roses – then the Vulgate cycle was an unhappy choice. The elaborately interlaced structure of the narrative as a whole was now so complex, so fraught with local significances, that subduing it to a single overall purpose was almost impossible. At times, therefore, in Malory's work, the whole story seems to be entangled completely in the hidden larger narrative of an unknowable destiny, in which the knight can only accept the necessity of 'going on adventure'; knights seem to be almost involuntary agents in the stories in which they act; stories split and fragment so that the whole landscape through which knights-errant move seems to be littered with the residues of narrative.[1]

This, along with an overwhelming sense of unhistoricalness and unrealness and the almost narcotic or balletic repetition of the rituals of jousting and fighting, is part of the dominant experience of reading Malory. But there is also a heroic quality in Malory's resistance to the single informing ideology of the Vulgate cycle – the theme that gave point to the apparent pointlessness of much of the action – namely, the nothingness of secular chivalry. In the Vulgate, the doom of the Round Table is written into the withholding of the Grail from the body of Arthurian knighthood as a whole. Camelot counts for nothing beside Corbenic and the whole system of secular chivalric idealism fades into nothingness in the transcendental light of a higher spirituality. Malory accepts the validity of religious experience, but still sees secular chivalry as the life of the great society here and now, and he refuses to see it nullified by the Grail. He resists that separation of planes of experience so characteristic of medieval Christian faith, and attempts instead to articulate a humanly intelligible narrative of the fall of the Round Table.

Lancelot is the focus of this powerful developing narrative: in him is centred the tragic division of loyalties that brings the world of Arthur to disaster. The working out of this pattern of intelligible process and human conflict is Malory's great triumph in the *Morte D'Arthur*. It was impossible for later writers not to be absorbed into, or forced into a reaction against, his account of things when they came to retell the Arthurian story.

Publication and Author

On 31 July 1485, William Caxton, who had introduced printing with moveable type into England only nine years before, published at his Westminster press a large volume in prose called *Le Morte D'Arthur*, which contained, as he said, the whole story of King Arthur and his knights of the Round Table. Caxton was a merchant of books, and his aim was to make money by putting into print those books that were marketable to an audience of upper- and middle-class readers already well established through the increasingly commercialized production of manuscript-books. His tastes were conservative, but he understood the movements of taste, and he knew that in France and Burgundy extended prose redactions of the older romances in prose and verse, designed for readers with leisure and money, had become fashionable. They fulfilled a desire on the part of such readers to have the great stories of the past – of Charlemagne and Guillaume d'Orange, of Troy and Jason and Godfrey of Boulogne – gathered compendiously into single compilations and written in a modern style. Caxton had already published a number of compilations of this kind based on French originals, and now he had on his hands something that might do for Arthur and the knights of the Round Table what the Burgundian compilers had done for Charlemagne and his paladins.

But Caxton was not only interested in making money, and his motives in this case seem to go deeper, as he expresses his desire to redeem a specifically English past. In his Preface to the *Morte D'Arthur* he tells how he had often been approached by 'many noble and divers gentlemen', who asked him why he had never put into print the story of the Grail and of Arthur. 'Noble and divers gentlemen' would often appear in Caxton's workshop asking him to do what he had already decided to do for good commercial reasons, and Caxton would fall in readily with their requests. As he says, Arthur has claims both in terms of his worthiness to be put in memory – he is after all the only Englishman among the Nine Worthy – and his assured historicity. For the latter, there is the evidence of his sepulchre at Glastonbury, Gawain's skull at Dover Castle, the Round Table at Winchester, and 'in other places Lancelot's sword and many other things'. It was a rebuke to the patriotic printer that Arthur seemed to be better known in foreign languages than in English.

> Wherefore, such as have late been drawn out briefly into English I have after the simple cunning that God hath sent me, under the favour and correction of all noble lords and gentlemen, enprised to imprint a book of the noble histories of the said King Arthur, and of certain of his knights, after a copy unto me delivered, which copy Sir Thomas Malory did take out of certain books of French, and reduced into English.

There follows Caxton's exhortation to the nobility of England to take note of the work and follow the example of the 'renowned acts of humanity, gentleness, and chivalries' that it affords:

> For herein may be seen noble chivalry, courtesy, humanity, friendliness, hardiness, love, friendship, cowardice, murder, hate, virtue, and

sin. Do after the good and leave the evil, and it shall bring you to good fame and renown.

Like many Englishmen of his time, Caxton professed to deplore the tarnished name of chivalry, in the aftermath of the Wars of the Roses (which ended when Richard III was killed at the battle of Bosworth Field in 1485 and Henry VII claimed the throne), and saw in the story of Arthur an image of a golden age which might serve as an exemplar to the present – or at least distract attention from its intractably unpleasant realities and make them easier to accept or forget about. One man who shared Caxton's profession of idealism, in what has been called this Indian summer of English chivalry,[2] was Sir Thomas Malory. This is how he gives expression to the idealized principles of the Round Table, at the holding of the first of the great feasts of Pentecost:

> Then the King established all the knights, and gave them riches and lands; and charged them never to do outrage nor murder, and always to flee treason, and to give mercy unto him that asketh mercy, upon pain of forfeiture of their worship and lordship of King Arthur for evermore; and always to do ladies, damosels, and gentlewomen and widows succour; strengthen them in their rights, and never to enforce them, upon pain of death. Also, that no man take no battles in a wrongful quarrel for no love, nor for no worldly goods. So unto this were all the knights sworn of the Table Round, both young and old. (III.15)

In a later passage, concerning love, Malory is even more explicit in his contrast of the past and the present, comparing faithful and fickle love, and how in the past men and women could be faithful lovers and no 'lecherous lusts' be between them, 'but nowadays men cannot love seven night but they must have all their desires' (XVIII.25).

There is apparently some slight discrepancy, as later scholars discovered, between Malory's knightly ideals and his own knightly career. If he is indeed the Sir Thomas Malory of Newbold Revell in Warwickshire (born about 1410) who bore the standard and turns of fortune of the earl of Warwick in the Wars of the Roses, then it would seem that he embarked at the age of about forty on an orgy of crime and violence of remarkable range and scope. He spent a good many of his last twenty years in prison (where he died in 1471), having been charged, amongst other things, with rape (of the same woman, twice), attempted murder (of the duke of Buckingham), sacrilege, cattle-stealing and blackmail. Whether this makes any difference to our view of his work is a question that is usually dismissed by saying that a person's life is irrelevant to that person's writing, but fortunately there is no great problem in this case, and no need to contrive explanations as to how a vicious and confirmed criminal came to write a nostalgic and idealized account of past chivalry. Malory's misfortune was to be on the wrong side at a crucial stage in the current Wars of the Roses; he was most likely charged with everything his accusers could think of in the hope that enough would stick to enable him to be put away for a long time, since he compounded the offence of being on the wrong side by failing to change sides, as did his master. It is perhaps a matter of 'Who painted the lion?' or, more specifically, 'In whose interests were the surviving records made?' As C. S. Lewis said, what should we think of Tristram if we had only had the evidence of King Mark's solicitors?[3]

It is an irony of the situation that Malory seems to have written all of his great work in prison, and indeed that imprisonment alone may have given him the leisure to write. Several of the explicits to individual books make it clear that the author is in prison (Caxton omits these marking divisions between books, and substitutes his own), and there is a paragraph in the story of Sir Tristram, when he is thrown into prison, which seems poignantly autobiographical:

> So Sir Tristram endured there great pain, for sickness had undertaken him, and that is the greatest pain a prisoner may have; for all the while a prisoner may have his health of body he may endure under the mercy of God and in hope of good deliverance. But when sickness toucheth a prisoner's body, then may a prisoner say all wealth is him bereft, and then he hath cause to wail and to weep. Right so did Sir Tristram when sickness had undertaken him, for then he took such sorrow that he had almost slain himself. (IX.36)

The Winchester Manuscript

It was a fair assumption that Malory's original manuscript had been through some editorial process at Caxton's hands, but the *Morte*

D'Arthur was known only in the version printed by Caxton until in 1934 a manuscript was discovered in Winchester College (now British Library MS Add. 59678) which clearly stood in a much closer relation to Malory's original. It showed that Caxton, in his desire to present Malory's work as the complete, continuous and definitive English version of the whole Arthurian story (as he explains in his Preface), had somewhat misrepresented the work by editing out internal text divisions and numbering the work in twenty-one books, broken up into chapters with new headings, and by thus obscuring the separateness of the original eight sections into which the work is divided in the Winchester manuscript. The precise nature of the relationship between the Winchester manuscript and Caxton's printed text is not as clear as this abbreviated account of his activities might suggest, since the Winchester manuscript, although it bears marks of printers' ink and was evidently once in a print-shop, was not Caxton's copy-text. Furthermore, changes that he appears to have made, such as the removal of much of the obtrusive alliteration that was taken over from the alliterative *Morte Arthure* in Book II of the Winchester manuscript, may have been made by Malory himself in a (lost) intermediate version.

The eight sections of the Winchester manuscript (which for convenience's sake will be called Books I–VIII from now on) deal with, respectively: (1) the birth of Arthur, his coming to the throne and early conquests, and the early adventures of the knights of the Round Table; (2) the war against Rome (drawn from the alliterative *Morte Arthure*); (3) the early adventures of Sir Lancelot; (4) Sir Gareth; (5) Sir Tristram; (6) the Grail; (7) the ill-fated love of Lancelot and Guenevere; and (8) the death of Arthur. Eugène Vinaver, whose life's work was to be the editing and explication of the Winchester manuscript, argued that the book structure revealed by the manuscript gave insight into Malory's essential originality as a narrative writer: what he had done was to unweave the interlaced strands of the Vulgate, with its polyphonic narrative of multitudes of parallel and interlocking adventures, and to draw out the tellable tales of single heroes, with a beginning, a directed movement, and an end. In other words, he invented the novel. Vinaver's arguments are pleasing and persuasive, and certainly borne out in the handling of the last two books, but there are many who would demur, pointing out that Malory takes great pleasure in interlaced narrative in Book I and in the enormously long Book V, which should not therefore be regarded as failures; that the books, though separate, are sequential, and build up powerfully to the telling of the one grand story of the rise, flourishing and fall of the Round Table; and that Malory works hard to bind the whole together by prophetic anticipation and backward reference, and also by the consistency with which he elevates Lancelot and concentrates upon him as both the epitome of chivalric idealism and the chief agent of its destruction. In all this, Malory does no more than follow up the hints in the vastly longer Vulgate or 'Lancelot-Graal' cycle.

Malory made direct use of two earlier English Arthurian poems, the alliterative *Morte Arthure* in Book II and the stanzaic *Morte Arthur* in the last two books. But his principal sources were the prose romances of the French Vulgate tradition, which as we have seen existed in three major groupings: the *Estoire de Merlin* and the *Suite du Merlin*; the *Tristan*; and the *Lancelot*, including the *Estoire del Saint Graal* and the *Mort Artu*. Malory's precise French sources, amidst the mass of variant versions, are not always easily identifiable, and it is possible at any point to underestimate or overestimate the degree to which he imposed upon the work as a whole his own ideas of pattern and structure. Generally speaking, though the evidence of his work on the English poems is that he is prepared to make clear choices about matters of disposition and emphasis, he does not make extensive changes in the given story material. His narrative techniques are correspondingly self-effacing, and characterized by simple but evocatively repetitive diction; stylized colloquial syntax and intonation; the minimum of descriptive visualization; expression of character through gesture, direct speech and dialogue rather than through analysis or comment; and very rare intervention by the narrator, and that mostly of a laconic and impersonal kind. Malory's success is less as an author than as the mediator through which the whole story of Arthur was written unforgettably into English prose.

Book I (Caxton's Books 1–4)

The first Book of the Winchester manuscript tells of Arthur's birth, the early marvels, the part played by Merlin, and Arthur's early battles to assert his overlordship; the tragic lives of Balin and Balan; the adventure of the white hart; and various quests involving Gawain, Torre, Pellinor, Uwain, Marhalt, and Pelleas and Ettard. Interwoven with these already complexly interlaced adventures are the stories of Merlin and his ill-fated love for Nineve, and of the treacherous intrigues of Morgan le Fay, Arthur's half-sister. Not to know exactly what is going on, or why particular knights act in the way they do, which we remember as the character of the Vulgate romances and of their predecessors among Chrétien's continuators, is very much the character of the narrative here as it follows on from the clear story of Arthur's establishment of his power. Within the structure of the *Morte D'Arthur* as a whole, it could be said to portray the 'learning curve' of knights such as Gawain and Pellinor as they are brought to learn the consequences of, respectively, accidentally cutting off a lady's head (III.7) and failing to rescue a damsel in evident distress (III.11). Arthur's own behaviour is at times brutal, and his encounters with women disconcertingly abrupt. So he meets Lionors, and

> set his love greatly upon her, and so did she upon him; and the King had ado with her and begot on her a child. And his name was Borre, that was after a good knight, and of the Table Round. (I.17)

And that's all we ever hear of her; in the next chapter, a week later, he falls in love with Guenevere (I.18), and in the next chapter after that he comes across Margawse, wife of King Lot of Orkney, and

> the King cast great love unto her, and desired to lie by her. And so they were agreed, and he begot upon her Sir Mordred, and she was sister on the mother's side, Igraine, unto Arthur. (I.19)

The declaration of the principles of the Round Table at the Pentecostal feast, already quoted, comes, significantly, at the end of this portion of the narrative.

Much remains enigmatic and mysterious, as knights are drawn into those kinds of adventure that have no apparent point or meaning but that are to be the imperative and life-blood of Arthurian romance. The presence of Merlin, a visitant from another narrative world, adds much to the air of mysteriousness. His omniscience, it is true, can be a trial: he appears on one occasion, quite gratuitously, in an impenetrable and ridiculous disguise so that Arthur will not recognize him

(I.17), and often sets Arthur conundrums that he is bound to get wrong. He asks Arthur, for instance, whether he prefers the sword or the scabbard he has just got for him. 'The sword', replies Arthur, quite reasonably. Merlin (triumphantly):

> 'Ye are the more unwise, for the scabbard is worth ten of the sword, for while ye have the scabbard upon you, ye shall lose no blood be ye never so sore wounded. Therefore keep well the scabbard always upon you.' (I.25)

'How was I supposed to know that?' one wishes Arthur had been able to reply. But it is Merlin's prescience that sets up the anticipatory forebodings that bind the narrative in the chain of inevitability. He foretells to Arthur of Pellinor that 'he shall tell you the name of your own son begotten of your sister that shall be the destruction of all this realm' (I.24) and warns him 'that Guenevere was not wholesome for him to take to wife, for he warned him that Lancelot should love her, and she him again' (III.1). Arthur has never heard of Lancelot at this point, but he is in any case destinally programmed not to listen to Merlin, except when, forewarned that Mordred shall be born on May-day, he has all the lords' sons born on that day set adrift on the sea to perish (I.27). Mordred of course is shipwrecked and saved and reappears many hundreds of pages later (IX.3) without a word further of explanation. It is at times like this that Malory's *Morte D'Arthur* is least like a novel and most like a narrative of portentous, prophetic and mysterious happenings, like the Old Testament.

Books II, III and IV (Caxton's Books 5–7)

These three books all together are still shorter than the sprawling Book I. Book II tells of Arthur's invasion of the continent after rejecting the emperor Lucius's demand for tribute, the fight with the giant of St Michael's Mount, and the conquest of France and Italy. It is based not on a French prose romance but on the English alliterative *Morte Arthure*. It is a reasonable assumption that it was the first of the tales to be written, and that Malory, having whetted his appetite for translation, turned subsequently to the French originals.

It may be important that his tastes should have been first formed by the English work – particularly for the effect it may have had on his concept of chivalry, which is more martial and heroic than the French, less courtly and religious. Malory throws in references here and there to his hero Lancelot and gives him a larger role in the invasion campaign. He also of course postpones the tragic ending of the *Morte Arthure,* and has Arthur crowned emperor in Rome before returning home in triumph to England (it will be from a different campaign that he will be later brought home from abroad to face Mordred).

Book III is an account of Sir Lancelot du Lake's early adventures before he becomes fatally entangled with Guenevere (though the liaison already seems common knowledge). The redisposition of material here, which is skilful and well controlled, perhaps reflects Malory's especial bias in wanting to present Lancelot, at least for a time, as the perfect knight rather than the perfect adulterer (the two things tended to be inseparable in the French). Lancelot is less interesting, it must be said, as the infallible fighting machine – who must for instance constantly fight in disguise because otherwise no one will dare to fight him – than as the later human and fallible figure torn between love and honour.

Book IV, the tale of Sir Gareth of Orkney, is one of Malory's triumphs. Not drawn directly from any known work, and likely to have more than usual of Malory's own invention, it is the familiar and favourite tale of the knight of apparently low birth (he is actually Gawain's brother) who proves his prowess in a series of increasingly difficult adventures, and so confounds the lady Lynette, who has scorned him from the moment he took up the quest. Such stories, with all the pleasure they give in the transformation of an unlikely kitchen lad, who only craves three square meals a day, into a superabundantly brave and gifted knight, rest upon a belief in innate gentility that sits oddly beside a myth much cultivated in the Middle Ages, that true worth is in a certain personal integrity and not in birth and breeding. The story of Sir Gareth is the first in which we encounter Malory's skill and subtlety in handling love-relationships and the finer points of social etiquette. The later part of the narrative lacks some of the impetus of the earlier, where the sharp exchanges of Gareth and Lynette build up irresistibly to the climax of the meeting with the Red Knight of the Red Launds (VII.17).

Book V, 'Sir Tristram of Lyones' (Caxton's Books 8–12)

The first four of the Winchester manuscript's eight books constitute nearly a third of the whole, but the one book of Sir Tristram is a good deal more than a third. The book has been thought a disappointment, in which Malory's technique of disentangling the tellable tale breaks down; he finds it impossible to isolate the story of Tristram and Isoude, and impossible on the other hand to handle full polyphonic narrative. There is plenty of vigour and fine writing, but the total effect, it is said, is one of incoherence.

Now it is true that the story of Tristram and Isoude, in its truncated form, lacks its full power: it is not Malory's purpose at this point to show the Round Table as anything but in its full glory, and certainly the second in pre-eminence of the knights of the Round Table cannot be allowed to die so inconsequentially before the introduction of the Grail has signalled the fateful onset of decline. Already deprived of its ending, the main story is itself the weaker version favoured in the French *Tristan*, in which King Mark is made into an out-and-out villain, in order to glorify Tristram, and Tristram and Isoude are in love long before they drink the potion. The story thus lacks much of the complexity and intensity of the traditional version represented in Gottfried's *Tristan*. However, the quality of the writing in Book V, the rich expression that it gives to the varieties and entertaining complexities of the chivalric code, are different from anything before, a world away from the saga-like qualities of Books I and II, and with a sophistication only adumbrated in Books III and IV. The precision of Tristram's understanding of the finer points of the code is why he is to be admired, for instance the knowledge he shows of the technical terms of hunting, which displays his innate gentility even before his royal birth has been revealed (VIII.3); or the fine sense of etiquette he shows when, even though he has quite recently been sleeping with the wife of Sir Segwardis, he must allow her husband the first opportunity of going to rescue her when she is carried off by Sir Bleoberis as the gift that King Mark had promised him (VIII.15).

But as Book V wears on, it does seem that Malory lost track a little of what he was doing; even Caxton gives eighty-eight chapters to his colossal Book 10, almost as if his mind was elsewhere. Though much of the story is about Tristram and Isoude, and many too of the finest passages, such as Tristram's wonderful ironic speech of farewell to Cornwall (IX.21), much is about the miscellaneous adventures of Palomides, Lamorak, Dinadan and others, in whom it is harder to sustain a keen interest, even though Palomides is at least unusual in being a Saracen, and Dinadan in being at times a comic anti-hero.

Various characters whom we think we remember emerge through the mists. One is Mordred, who plays a more or less normal role, even a respectable one. Everyone seems to have forgotten who he is, including Malory. Probably Malory went back to Book I and laced it with Merlin's prophecies of Arthur's death at the hands of Mordred and the fall of the Round Table in order to give an appropriate sense of destiny and foreshadowing, but found it too much or never got round to do anything similar in the vast book of Tristram. Towards the end, the pace quickens: there is the first introduction of the Grail (XI.2), and following that the conceiving of Galahad, when Lancelot is led to what he thinks is Guenevere's bed but is in fact Elaine's (XI.8). It is an episode that could be called 'The Mistakes of a Night', and the potential comedy of the scene is left marvellously unrealized in Malory's circumstantial narration, but it is an event of momentous import. Galahad's conception must be surrounded with mystery so that it may be the fulfilment of a hidden destiny unknown to his father, like the conceptions of Arthur and Mordred. Lancelot must be tricked into symbolically giving up his virtue and power to his son; he is merely the factor through which chivalric pre-eminence has been engrossed so that Galahad can take it from him and show it to be worthless.

Book VI, 'The Tale of the Sankgreal' (Caxton's Books 13–17)

This book is largely a translation of the *Queste del Saint Graal*, but Malory manages nevertheless to give the impression that he is interested in some things more than others, in Lancelot's failure more than Galahad's success. Malory's attachment to the world and his respect for secular chivalry, his refusal to accept the nothingness of secular chivalry set beside spiritual chivalry, his tendency to treat the Grail as a magical object rather than as the bearer of mystical communion with Christ, involves some devaluation of the Grail imagery.

He also shows a characteristic tendency to transform otherworldly transcendental mysticism into worldly morality, and a preference for the ethical over the spiritual, for which the French sometimes gives him warrant, as when Gawain is reproved by a hermit because he has been a bad knight, not because he has been a knight (XIII.16).

The Grail story is different from the others. Where it seemed before that nothing was explained, here everything is explained, over and over again. Behind every bush and under every tree there is a hermit or similarly qualified person waiting to explain the significance of everything that has been happening, and at the same time to throw in expositions of key points of Christian doctrine (for example, XIII.12). Allegory for the first time rears its head, as for instance when Gawain has it explained to him how 'the Castle of Maidens betokeneth the good souls that were in prison before the Incarnation of Our Lord Jesu Christ' (XIII.16). It is elsewhere explained how the Round Table symbolizes the world, as being the image of all that men want in the way of worldly renown (XIV.2). It is therefore an apt symbol of what men should not seek. Poor Lancelot: coming across a fight between a large number of white knights and a smaller number of black knights, he naturally joins the battle on the side of the black knights in accord with the tenets of chivalry and does marvellous deeds of chivalry (XV.5). But he cannot beat them, and he slinks off into the forest, sure that since he hasn't won he must be even more sinful than he thought. Inevitably he comes upon a chapel, where a woman recluse explains how his pride caused him to misunderstand everything (XV.6). The black knights are sinners and the white betoken virginity and chastity. Fighting now requires a supernatural sanction, otherwise you cannot win.

But throughout, Malory seeks to mitigate Lancelot's failing, even to suggest that he had a partial sight of the Grail. His more characteristic view of his hero comes just before the climactic meeting with Galahad, when Lancelot comes ashore from a ship which has borne him mysteriously for a month, fed only by the eucharist and accompanied only by the dead body of Sir Perceval's sister.

> And so on a night he went to play him by the water's side, for he was somewhat weary of the ship. (XVII.13)

There seems some assertion of the irredeemably and obstinately human in Lancelot's growing weary of the ship. To grow weary of having all

one's bodily and spiritual needs supplied by the eucharist and in
having as one's sole companion the dead body of one's friend's sister
shows some lack of spirituality.

Books VII and VIII (Caxton's Books 18–21)

The two last books are closely linked, and are usually regarded as
Malory's greatest achievement. Book VII, 'Lancelot and Guenevere',
tells of the return from the quest of the Grail, the return of Lancelot to
Guenevere, the accusations of Sir Mador de la Porte against her that
she poisoned a knight at one of her feasts, the defeat of Sir Mador by
Guenevere's champion, Lancelot, the episode of the fair maid of Astolat,
Guenevere's jealousy, Lancelot's madness, and finally the episode first
recounted by Chrétien where Meliagaunt, after kidnapping Guenevere,
accuses her of adultery with numerous unnamed knights and Lancelot
comes to the rescue yet again. Book VIII, 'The Death of Arthur',
recounts the plots of Agravain and Mordred and the condemnation of
Guenevere for adultery; Lancelot rescues her from the stake, at the
last minute, but in rescuing her accidentally kills Gareth, Gawain's
brother; Gawain vows vengeance, the wars of Arthur and Gawain
against Lancelot begin, and after the surrender of Guenevere to the
king, Arthur and Gawain pursue Lancelot into France, where news
of the treachery of Mordred arrives. There follow the last battle, the
death of Arthur, and the retirement of Guenevere and Lancelot into
nunnery and monastery, respectively.

The Romance of Adventure

Various events in fifteenth-century history and the Wars of the Roses
can be plausibly associated with episodes in the *Morte d'Arthur*, and
indeed the whole enterprise of the Round Table can be regarded, in
political terms, as a kind of 'chivalric policing' or 'chivalric peace-
keeping'.[4] Malory does occasionally make reference to his own present
day, in the broadest terms, lamenting for instance the ease with which
Mordred was able to seduce the barony of England from their allegiance to the noble King Arthur, and commenting:

> Lo, thus was the old custom and usages of this land; and men say that
> we of this land have not yet lost that custom. Alas, this is a great
> default of us Englishmen, for there may nothing please us no term.
> (XXI.1)

This is a bitterly felt reflection, coming from a follower of the Lancas-
trian cause. But the dominant impression of the work, except for
Book II, which has a different origin as part of the national epic, is not
of an attempt at an allegory or critique of contemporary historical and
political realities but of the creation of a world which will act by its
very remoteness as a criticism of the modern world.

The world of chivalric adventure in Malory, as in the French prose
romances that inspired him, is a world remote and unreal in place
and time. It is Logres, a never-existent England in the past, a land of
forests to ride through and castles to stay the night in, and every so
often 'a hermitage was under a wood, and a great cliff on the other
side, and a fair water running under it' (XVIII.16). Mention of particular places, as when Lancelot makes his horse swim over the Thames
to Lambeth (XIX.4), produces an incongruous effect. Malory has too a
kind of scrupulous-sounding specificness – speaking for instance of
Camelot, 'that is in English called Winchester' (XII.10), or Ascolat,
'that is in English Guildford' (XVIII.8), or debating whether Joyous
Gard is Alnwick or Bamborough (XXI.12) – which works bizarrely to
reinforce the sense of remoteness from reality, the concessions to the
mundane acting as the guarantor of the romance 'contract' with the
reader. Time too is also strangely both specific and unspecific. We are
given a date, AD 454, for the occupation of the Siege Perilous (XIII.2),
but anachronisms abound (they are the rule): the Romans demand
tribute, but England is Christian and full of hermitages; the Tower of
London is already there for Guenevere to retire to, but Lancelot we
are also told is ninth in the immediate line of descent from Joseph of
Arimathaea.

Most obvious of all is the remoteness from reality as more generally
defined in terms of the removal of the story from the usual con-
straints that people live under. It is a surprise to us when Malory tells
us that 'much people drew unto Sir Mordred' (XXI.1). 'People' do not
usually figure in the narrative, and it seems that Mordred is taking an
unfair advantage in recruiting them. The absence of this whole class

of 'people', with all their interests and concerns, is one of the 'givens' of the romance-narrative of adventure. The sense of class is omnipresent: Priamus's main worry, after being defeated and apparently mortally wounded by the disguised Gawain, is that his vanquisher should be of birth adequate to allow him to die happy (V.10), and one of the sure signs of Gareth's lowly origin to the lady Lynette is that when he is granted a boon at the court of Arthur, he asks for twelve months' board and lodging (VII.1). Such plebeian considerations are not the concern of a true knight, for whom food and drink are ceremonial matters only.

For the most part, with the obvious exceptions (for instance, Book II), the adventures are not connected with territorial or dynastic ambitions, the usual reasons for fighting in real life, but are self-sufficient as displays and testings of the chivalric virtues of prowess and courtesy. The characteristic pattern is of the knight riding forth to seek adventures, for no reason at all:

> Thus Sir Launcelot rested him long with play and game; and then he thought to prove himself in strange adventures, and bade his nephew, Sir Lionel, for to make him ready, 'for we must go seek adventures'. So they mounted on their horses, armed at all rights, and rode into a deep forest and so into a plain. (VI.1)

Lionel does not reply, as he might have done in real life, 'Where are we going? How long will we be away?' but just gets on his horse. Fortunately, the forests are full of adventures, and in no time at all our knight will be ware of a knight chasing another knight or a lady or him, or a brachet chasing a hart, or a knight unarmed weeping beside a well. Malory's economy of method sometimes makes the encounters seem a little arbitrary, as when Sir Tristram and Sir Palomides come upon a knight sleeping and awaken him.

> And so the knight arose up hastily and put his helm upon his head and gat a great spear in his hand; and without any more he hurled unto Sir Tristram, and smote him clean from his saddle to the earth. (X.2, Caxton)

It is, of course, Lancelot.

The repetitive formality of the pattern of meeting, challenge, joust with spear, fight on foot with sword, is as strict as the steps of a dance, whatever reality it may have had being choreographed now into a ballet of violence.[5] Occasional variation is introduced when every so often the mysterious Questing Beast, who makes a noise in his stomach like thirty couple of questing hounds, will race across the foreground with Sir Palomides in hot pursuit, like an eccentric lepidopterist in a stage farce rushing across with his butterfly net. Palomides inherits the quest from Pellinor (I.19), and pursues it still many hundreds of pages later (X.13). No reason is given.

> This beast evermore Sir Palomides followed, for it was called his quest.
> (IX.12)

The Questing Beast is a prime example of what might be called the imperfect assimilation of given story materials to Malory's intentions, whatever they were, and assuming that at any particular point he had any.

Obeying the formal imperative of 'going out on adventure', the knight must prove his worth, his 'worship', through prowess, courtesy and unfailing dedication to the service of women. These are the qualities that Lancelot above all epitomizes. There is much concern, first of all, with prowess, and the 'prowess-rankings' are a staple topic of conversation when one knight meets another. So Sir Tristram, in disguise, disagrees with his host's estimate that Sir Gawain is a better knight than Sir Gaheris.

> 'That is not so,' said Sir Tristram, 'for I have met with them both, and I felt Sir Gaheris for the better knight, and Sir Lamorak, I call him as good as any of them except Sir Launcelot.'
> 'Why name ye not Sir Tristram?' said his host, 'For I account him as good as any of them.'
> 'I know not Sir Tristram,' said Sir Tristram. (IX.42, Caxton)

But in the design of the work as a whole Malory uses this concern for the rankings to display the pre-eminence of three knights, Lancelot, Tristram and Lamorak, and the supreme pre-eminence of Lancelot, so that when the time comes for him to bear the full weight of the tragic ending of the story he has been built up into a surpassing hero.

Beyond simple prowess is another more complex quality, courtesy, that nobility or generosity of temper which prompts a knight always to respect women, never to take mean advantage of another knight, always to dismount promptly when an opponent has been unhorsed, never to prey upon the weak – as does Sir Breuse sans Pitie, one of the few personages who, despite all Malory's efforts to disentangle the threads of the narrative, makes a posthumous reappearance. It is the quality displayed by Tristram and Lamorak, when they fight together all day and finally each acknowledge the other the victor and vow never to fight each other again (IX.11). Above all, though, of course, it is Lancelot's prerogative. At the tournaments Lancelot, disguised, always waits to see which is the weaker side before joining in (this is the irony of his error in the quest of the Grail), and towards a brave and noble adversary he always displays a voluntary restraint of power for which Malory's favourite word is forbearance. When the young Gareth has fought bravely in the tournament, and Arthur calls upon his champion Lancelot to take on the new victor, Lancelot replies:

> 'Sir,' said Lancelot, 'I may well find in my heart for to forbear him as at this time, for he hath had travail enough this day. And when a good knight doth so well upon some day, it is no good knight's part to let him of his worship. . . . And therefore,' said Sir Lancelot, 'as for me, this day he shall have the honour; though it lay in my power to put him from it, yet would I not.' (VII.28)

Sometimes the challenge to courtesy is difficult to meet. When Guenevere demands the death of the slanderous Meliagaunt whom he has vanquished in battle and who has begged for mercy, Lancelot must and yet cannot accede. His solution is to fight with one side unarmed and one hand tied behind his back – and of course he wins (XIX.9). The perfectness of Lancelot's courtesy is demonstrated when he refuses Bors' invitation to him to kill Arthur in the final siege of Benwick:

> 'My lord the king, for God's love stint this strife, for ye get here no worship and I would do my utterance [if I were to do my utmost]. But always I forbear you, and ye nor none of yours forbear not me. And therefore, my lord, I pray you remember what I have done in many places, and now am I evil rewarded.'
>
> So when King Arthur was on horseback he looked on Sir Lancelot; then the tears burst out of his eyes, thinking of the great courtesy that was in Sir Lancelot more than in any other man. (XX.13)

The fineness of this courtesy, this voluntary rejection of what might more profitably serve the self and its appetite for survival, is a specifically medieval contribution to the ideal of the hero, one which King Alfred would not have understood, and quite different from the cool, laconic nonchalance of the Icelandic saga-heroes. It is the heroism of a Gary Cooper or a James Stewart rather than a Clint Eastwood.

With all this, the true knight must also be a true lover. There is of course little treatment of love itself as a psychological phenomenon, except fitfully with Lancelot and Tristram, and mostly it operates in the narrative as a fairly swiftly applied glue that unites man and woman for ever. The knight sets eyes on a lady and is 'so enamoured upon her that he wist not whether he were on horseback or on foot' (X.39):

> Then she unwimpled her visage. And when he saw her, he said, 'Here have I found my love and my lady.' (X.39)

The force of love is an inertial guidance system that directs the knight in his apparently motiveless and random adventures. But Malory himself is ambiguous about love. In the early books, especially in the Tale of Sir Lancelot, Malory selects from his material so as to concentrate on Lancelot's greatness as a warrior, not as a lover, and even gives to Lancelot a discourse on love and marriage which seems strangely at odds with his own admitted love for Guenevere. In response to a maid's questions about his lack of a wife and the rumour of his liaison with Guenevere, he replies:

> 'Fair damosel, I may not warn people to speak of me what it pleaseth them; but for to be a wedded man, I think it not; for then I must couch with her, and leave arms and tournaments, battles and adventures. And as for to say to take my pleasance with paramours, that will I refuse, in principal for dread of God. For knights that be adventurous should not be adulterers nor lecherous, for then they be not happy nor fortunate unto the wars. . . . And so who that useth paramours shall be unhappy, and all thing unhappy that is about them.' (VI.10)

There is dramatic irony here, but almost a suspicion that Malory is trying to postpone the recognition of Lancelot's adultery. He shows a similar uneasiness with Tristram and Isoude, as if unwilling to admit

the fact of adultery: he puts a peculiarly ambiguous defence of Tristram
into the mouth of the blameless Sir Perceval, who reproaches King
Mark thus for thinking ill of his nephew:

> 'Ye should never think that so noble a knight as Sir Tristram is, that he
> would do himself so great a villainy to hold his uncle's wife; howbeit,
> he may love your queen sinless, because she is called one of the fairest
> ladies of the world.' (X.51)

The causal relation of the last two clauses is interesting.

An interesting feature of the book of Tristram is the introduction
of the anti-lover, Sir Dinadan, who is respected for his prowess but
who is no servant of love. Tristram cannot accept this, for, he says, 'a
knight may never be of prowess but if he be a lover' (X.55), but
Dinadan, in answering Isoude's later reproach, explains his motives
perfectly clearly:

> 'Why,' said La Belle Isode, 'are ye a knight and are no lover? For sooth,
> it is a great shame to you; wherefore ye may not be called a good
> knight by reason but if ye make a quarrel for a lady.'
>   'God defend me,' said Sir Dinadan, 'for the joy of love is too short,
> and the sorrow thereof is duras over long.' (X.56)

Dinadan is anti-heroic in other respects too. When he and Tristram
come upon a knight matched against thirty, he refuses such an
unequal combat and is only prevailed upon after much grumbling
about having got into such a fireball's company (IX.22). Another
time, when he is called upon to observe the custom of the castle and
to joust for his night's lodging, he comments wearily, 'There is shrewd
harbour' (IX.23). 'It's been a hard day,' one hears him say. 'Perhaps
we could try the next castle.' Of course he does fight and acquit
himself well, but the protest is made, and Dinadan serves an important purpose in romance, that is, to encapsulate the anti-romantic
mockery so that it is contained within the romance and made to seem
ludicrous, not imposed from outside by the sceptical reader. It is
'concessionary comedy': by making a concession to scepticism, the
reader's agreement to the 'romance contract' is secured. It is, though,
a very small concession that Malory makes. Humour is not his strong
point.

The Tragedy of Lancelot

The familiar features of the medieval Arthurian romance of adventure achieve in Malory a special richness of expression, but for him the story of Arthur is more than a romance. Chivalry he regards as a serious political and moral ideal, a temporal expression of timeless virtues, and the destruction of that chivalry, and the downfall of the Round Table, are the matter of tragedy. Malory's last two books are not just an elegy on a world that has passed with the inevitable transience of all worldly things but an attempt to make the passing of that world intelligible. In retrospect, the justification of 'the whole book' is that it has shown us this world in its beginnings, its growth, its maturity and its full glory so that the full tragedy of its fall can now be appreciated. More than an interwoven tapestry of adventures, in which no one important is ever written out of the script, the *Morte D'Arthur* as a whole becomes a specific tract of experience, in time, with a beginning and an end, in death. The centre of this developing theme is Lancelot, in whom the tragic division of loyalties – loyalty to his lord and loyalty to Guenevere – is centred, and it is from this division that the downfall of the whole system directly proceeds.

The drawing out of this pattern of intelligible process and human conflict is Malory's great strength and special achievement, and a way of treating the story significantly different from the French originals. In the French prose *Lancelot*, the doom of the Round Table is written into the withholding of the Grail from the body of Arthurian knighthood as a whole. The ideals of secular chivalry are hollow at the core; systems of governance that attach themselves to the desires and ambitions of the fallen material world, however apparently noble in themselves, are inevitably transient. Lancelot's adultery was the trigger but not the cause of the destruction of the Round Table. Malory struggles not to recognize this clearly, preferring a version of events in which an intrinsically noble ideal world of secular chivalry was compromised and then destroyed by avoidable human weaknesses in its human members. He attempts to articulate a humanly intelligible narrative of the fall of the Round Table in which it will be not a lesson in Christian morality but an exploration of irresolvable human dilemmas of moral conduct.

Lancelot is built up from the beginning as the major figure, as he is in the Vulgate cycle. Even before he appears he is being surrounded with an aura of superlative pre-eminence (II.19), and in Merlin's prophecies of Lancelot's love for Guenevere there is a foreshadowing of the final disaster (III.1). Malory gives Lancelot a prominent place in the Tale of King Arthur's wars against the emperor Lucius, where in the English alliterative poem which here is Malory's source he does not appear at all. All through the tales of Gareth and Tristram, Lancelot is the pivot upon which all revolves, and the exemplar of chivalric idealism. Even in the story of the Grail, Lancelot is the centre of attention, even though it is Galahad who is the exemplar of the new spiritual chivalry. Lancelot's struggles and failures and half-repentances, his attachment to the material world the transitoriness and nothingness of which it was the purpose of the Grail to reveal, are still the main interest. But though Malory refuses the full spiritual implications of the failure in the Grail – that Lancelot and the Round Table are doomed – nevertheless the return of the knights from the quest of the Grail forces into the open the moral implications of Lancelot's love for Guenevere – not the fact of adultery but the disloyalty to Arthur that is its consequence, or at least the consequence of its being brought into the open. Arthur is reluctant to act when Agravain first voices his suspicions:

> For as the French book saith, the King was full loath that such a noise should be upon Sir Lancelot and his queen. For the King had a deeming of it; but he would not hear thereof, for Sir Lancelot had done so much for him and for the Queen so many times that, wit you well, the King loved him passingly well. (XX.2)

It is characteristic of Malory that when the interpretation of events is enigmatic, and motives are hidden or ambiguous, he will assign his narratorial comments to 'the French book'. There is nothing of this in any known French book, and we are left to guess whether Arthur is making a practical calculation of what he stands to lose or gain, or whether his reluctance to act on his own suspicions (his 'deeming') is a mark of his trustfulness and perhaps of the trustworthiness of those in whom he places his trust, or whether he simply does not want to rock the boat.

The Book of Lancelot and Guenevere, following the return of the knights from the Grail quest, shows us the gradual binding of Lancelot into the toils of his dilemma, and is introduced with ominous warnings,

in which Malory, with the due distance of 'as the book saith', follows
his French sources:

> Then, as the book saith, Sir Lancelot began to resort unto Queen
> Guinevere again, and forgot the promise and the perfection that he
> made in the quest. For, as the book saith, had not Sir Lancelot been in
> his privy thoughts and in his mind so set inwardly to the Queen as he
> was in seeming outward to God, there had no knight passed him in the
> quest of the Sangrail, but ever his thoughts were privily on the Queen.
> (XVIII.1)

Lancelot is now placed in increasingly difficult and eventually impossible situations. There are three stages: first, he defends Guenevere
against the accusations of Sir Mador de la Porte that she had his brother
poisoned at her feast, accusations which we know to be untrue; and
then, secondly, against the accusations of Meliagaunt that the blood
in Guenevere's bed proved that she had slept with an unnamed
wounded knight of her entourage, accusations that were false, but
only in the letter (the blood was actually Lancelot's). His recognition
of the ambiguity of his position is not in anything he says – it is not
Malory's way to allow us to enter the inner life of his characters in
that way – but in a gesture that speaks even more eloquently. It is in
the episode of the healing of Sir Urre (Malory's own invention, which
he uses also as an opportunity to do a roll-call of the knights of the
Round Table and tell us finally what happened to Tristram, XIX.11),
where after all 110 knights have unsuccessfully 'searched' the wounds
of poor Sir Urre, who can only be healed by the best knight in the
world, Lancelot happens by. Showing much reluctance, he is prevailed upon by Arthur to make the attempt, and in his searching of
the seven wounds they are healed:

> Then King Arthur and all the kings and knights kneeled down and gave
> thankings and lovings [praises] unto God and unto His Blessed Mother.
> And ever Sir Lancelot wept as he had been a child that had been
> beaten. (XIX.12)

It is a moment of complex, even impenetrable significance, though
we know that Lancelot is both honoured and shamed, and we know
he knows it. Lancelot feels himself reproved by the honour bestowed

upon him; it is a falsehood, and he is practising upon the trusting honesty of Arthur – or of God, like Isolde in the episode of the ordeal when Jesus becomes complicit like 'a windblown sleeve'.

But finally, the slanders against which he has to defend Guenevere – that she was untrue to her lord with person or persons unspecified – are, as he knows, true. He must defend her, out of loyalty to her, but the defence involves outright defiance of his lord and, by symbolic accident, the slaying of the knight who loves and owes him most, Sir Gareth, and the earning of Gawain's perpetual enmity (Gawain grows suddenly from being a playboy to being an implacable and dangerous enemy). Still Lancelot thinks he can solve all problems with his sword, thus reversing the proposition on which the rule of Arthur has been based: it is not now that right gives victory to the good cause but that might proves the cause good. As he waits unarmed in Guenevere's bedroom for the onrush of Agravain and his posse, it is his lack of armour that Lancelot laments, not the shame of what he has done nor even of being caught:

> 'Well, madam,' said Sir Lancelot, 'sith it is so that the day is come that our love must depart, wit you well I shall sell my life as dear as I may. And a thousandfold,' said Sir Lancelot, 'I am more heavier for you than for myself. And now I had liever than to be lord of all Christendom that I had sure armour upon me, that men might speak of my deeds or [before] ever I were slain.' (XX.3)

Malory has an enigmatic aside in this scene, in which he echoes what he said earlier about true and faithful love and seems to be trying to suggest that it is the modern mind alone that thinks the relationship of Lancelot and Guenevere adulterous:

> And so lightly he was had into the chamber; for as the French book saith, the Queen and Sir Lancelot were together. And whether they were abed or at other manner of disports, me list not thereof make no mention, for love that time was not as love is nowadays. (XX.3)

In the earlier scene in which Queen Guenevere goes maying in springtime, Malory sets up an elaborate and not entirely intelligible parallel between love and the seasons, between the flourishing of love in the springtime and the fading of love with the coming of winter. He speaks of the former as true and stable, the latter as the fickle and transient love that characterizes modern times. He seems to wish to associate the love of Lancelot and Guenevere with the true and chaste love that was of old – they are insinuated to be its unnamed practitioners – yet the seasonal parallel he chooses makes the association inevitably ambiguous, while the impossibility of doing any more than insinuate that their love was true and chaste (since it has been shown that it wasn't) leaves only the fallback position that at least their love was an example of 'stability' – which in its turn might be construed as persistence in misdemeanour. It is a puzzling passage, and the allusion to it in the climactic scene of the bedroom ambush does not make anything clearer. Nor is this the first time that Malory has used the fiction of 'the French book' to enigmatize and evade the consequences of his own narrative. What he seems to want is for the tragic fall to pivot on a clash of equal loyalties within Lancelot, but finds it difficult to see adulterous love and loyalty to one's lord as equal obligations. So he clouds the issue with hints and doubts, his strategies aided as always by his reticence concerning the inner life of his characters. A screen is thrown up between the reader and the private motives of the characters, amid a pretence that no distinction needs to be made between public and private behaviour. Yet it is clear that they are different – indeed, as has been said, 'it is the intrusion of the private into the public which forms the basis of the tragedy'.[6]

Malory's conspiracy with Lancelot in the attempt at obscuring or ambiguating his offence can however be no more than a temporary and superficial palliative. His defence of his actions before Arthur involves him in temporizing (which is little different from lying) and in committing the proof of the accusation of adultery to his own force of arms, which he knows to be unassailable. It was true, strictly, to answer Meliagaunt's accusations:

> 'I say nay plainly, that this night there lay none of these ten knights wounded with my lady Queen Guenivere; and that I will prove with my hands, that ye say untruly in that.' (XIX.7)

By contrast, the specious untruth or logic-chopping of his later answer is bitterly evident:

'If there be any knight . . . that will say or dare say but that she is true
and clean to you, I here myself, Sir Lancelot du Lake, will make it good
upon his body that she is a true lady unto you.' (XX.15)

In the end it is Lancelot himself who is the victim of the forces he has
set in train. He restores Guenevere to Arthur at the request of the
pope, but Gawain's desire for revenge for the killing of Gareth cannot
be assuaged and he draws Arthur off to the siege of Lancelot's castle
at Benwick, in France, which leaves England open for Mordred's seizure
of power. The day of destiny arrives, the last battle, and the fearful
symbolic death of Arthur and Mordred at each other's hands:

And when Sir Mordred felt that he had his death's wound, he thrust
himself with the might that he had up to the bur [butt] of King Arthur's
spear; and right so he smote his father, King Arthur, with his sword
holding in both his hands, upon the side of the head, that the sword
pierced the helmet and the tay [outer layer] of the brain. And there-
with Mordred dashed down stark dead to the earth. (XXI.4)

Night falls, and by the moonlight Sir Lucan sees the battlefield as the
robbers and spoilers get to work on the corpses. The reign of darkness
resumes, it seems, and Arthur is carried away.

The concentration of the narrative upon the ancient and tragic
story of the death of Arthur temporarily displaces Lancelot, and his
final meeting with Guenevere, now the abbess of a nunnery, has a
posthumous air (XXI.10). It is time now for Lancelot's sanctification
and his final acceptance, when all else is gone, of the superiority of
the life of the monastic makers of his story. He endures long in
penance, prayers and fastings, and dies in an odour of sanctity. But
this is not Malory's ending. After all the pieties, Malory gives the last
words to Sir Ector, who arrives to find Lancelot dead, and speaks his
elegy over his brother's body:

'Ah, Lancelot,' he said, 'thou were head of all Christian knights! And
now I dare say,' said Sir Ector, 'thou, Sir Lancelot, there thou liest, that
thou were never matched of earthly knight's hand. And thou were the
courteousest knight that ever bore shield; and thou were the truest
friend to thy lover that ever bestrode horse; and thou were the truest
lover of a sinful man that ever loved woman; and thou were the kindest
man that ever struck with sword; and thou were the goodliest person

that ever came among press of knights. And thou was the meekest man and the gentlest that ever ate in hall among ladies, and thou were the sternest knight to thy mortal foe that ever put spear in the rest.' Then there was weeping and dolour out of measure. (XXI.13)

His praise of Lancelot, significantly, is couched entirely in the terms of secular chivalry according to which Lancelot had lived.

6

The Arthurian Sleep and the Romantic Revival: Tennyson's *Idylls of the King*

The year 1485 was the high point in the English history of Arthur. Not only did Caxton publish Malory's *Morte D'Arthur* in that year, but there succeeded to the throne a dynasty, the Tudors, who had Welsh ancestry and who claimed descent ultimately from Arthur. Arthur was still a potent political figure, capable of symbolizing national re-generation. Richard III had accused Henry of being an upstart, with no claim to the throne (the Tudor claim was, in truth, somewhat unusual); so Henry had genealogists prove that he was descended from Arthur, and from Brutus too, for good measure. He called his first son, born in 1486, 'Arturus secundus'. Unfortunately, the young prince died before his father, and England had to face the future with Henry VIII.

But, for many reasons, Arthurian literature was starting to go into decline. Arthurian like other chivalric romances had lost whatever historical roots they had once remotely had, with the idealized knight of the feudal retinue giving way to more politically self-conscious figures such as the idealized Tudor governor and Renaissance gen-tleman. Romances also came under the Protestant lash, as in *The Scholemaster* (1570) of Roger Ascham, who was at one time tutor to the young Princess Elizabeth:

In our forefathers tyme, whan Papistrie, as a standyng poole, covered and overflowed all England, fewe bookes were read in our tong, savyng certaine bookes of Chevalrie, as they sayd, for pastime and pleasure, whiche, as some say, were made in Monasteries, by idle Monkes, or wanton Chanons; as one for example, *Morte Arthure*: the whole pleasure of which booke standeth in two speciall poyntes, in open mansslaughter and bold bawdrye: in which booke those be counted the noblest Knightes that do kill most men without any quarell, and commit fowlest advoulteries by sutlest shiftes: as Sir Launcelote with the wife of King Arthure his master: Syr Tristram with the wife of King Marke his uncle: Syr Lamerocke with the wife of King Lote, that was his owne aunte. This is good stuffe, for wise men to laugh at, or honest men to take pleasure at.

Ascham gives a wildly inaccurate account of pre-Reformation literacy and reading practice, but as long as he can abuse Malory's *Morte D'Arthur* as both immoral *and* Catholic, and immoral because Catholic, he is content.

Many romances stayed in print, but they fell off after 1575, partly being replaced by the new Spanish romances, partly through being scorned as they declined into ballad, broadside, and popular and children's writing. The need that Arthur had served as a vehicle for political purposes was now met from other historical sources deemed to be more authentic (there was much debate about the historicity of Arthur), including Geoffrey of Monmouth. Geoffrey's *Historia* had something of a revival, inspiring not only the irretrievably lost and inimitably titled play of *Mulmutius Dunwallow* by William Rankins but also *The True Chronicle History of King Leir* (1594), the ancestor of Shakespeare's play. As to Arthur himself, and the Arthurian story, Shakespeare's allusions, in their generally comic context, suggest that, like Chaucer, he viewed the legend with good-natured contempt, or at least did not regard it seriously.[1]

There was another problem. The sixteenth century had begun to be troubled by the easy commerce that the Middle Ages had maintained between fact and fiction. Often it seemed to them that the Middle Ages made light of a distinction that was becoming fundamental to their perception, as it was being shaped by the new science and by writers like Francis Bacon. Their anxiety may have been fuelled by discoveries in the New World of actual places more fabulous than those formerly fabled, so that a new and more secure barrier between fact and fiction had to be erected. Exploration in the Indies and America made Arthurian romance seem flat and old-fashioned; if fabling was wanted, reality could supply it better than any fable; if history was wanted, this was not history.

Edmund Spenser

Arthur, since he could not be historical, or fact, had now to become fiction. This is what Spenser does: he makes Arthur more completely a figure of romance by removing him completely from his history, acknowledging that he is dead, and giving him a completely new quest and a completely new lady – the Faerie Queene. In this manner he trades up the value of Arthur's name whilst giving him a new identity as the allegorical embodiment of all the chivalric, martial and personal virtues that the heroes of the different books of *The Faerie Queene* (1589, 1596) individually personify. Prince Arthur's quest for Gloriana, the Faerie Queene (which is prompted, in true medieval style, by a dream he has of her), also figures forth, in polite courtly manner, the prostration of the poet-petitioner before the inaccessible glory of the Virgin Queen, or the similar prostration of any discreetly unnamed court personage (Spenser did go so far as to suggest, in the letter to Sir Walter Ralegh prefixed to the poem, that Ralegh's devotion to the queen was alluded to in the love's service of Arthur's squire, Timias, to Belphoebe), and above all the dedication of the nation, personified in Arthur, to their queen.

From time to time therefore, though understandably he never achieves or even finds the Faerie Queene, Arthur turns up to help out others in moments of particular distress. In Book I, Canto 7, he makes his first appearance, bearing on his helmet the crest of Uther Pendragon –

> His haughtie helmet, horrid all with gold,
> Both glorious brightnesse, and great terrour bred;
> For all the crest a Dragon did enfold
> With greedie pawes, and ouer all did spred
> His golden wings . . .
>
> (I.vii.stanza 31) –

and carrying the shield, sword and armour wrought by Merlin. He fights at Una's request against the giant Orgoglio and the wicked Duessa, who have captured the Red Cross Knight, and defeats these like all enemies with the inevitability of one who bears not only the image of his divine Lady on his baldric but also a shield which cannot be pierced by any weapon and which moreover will blind, petrify or pulverize any enemy who looks upon it. Arthur makes half-a-dozen further appearances, still engaged obscurely on his quest for the Faerie Queene, often in the company of beautiful distressed damsels; he kills the giant Corflambo, rescues the warrior-lady Britomart, and drifts in and out of the story. Apart from the paraphernalia that has been mentioned, Spenser's Arthur has almost nothing to do with the Arthur of tradition.

Arthur in the Seventeenth Century

Though it was not for a while a major source of inspiration to imaginative writers, the Arthurian story continued to have a political significance. The Tudor propaganda of Arthurian descent was handed down to the Stuarts (James I was hailed as the returned Arthur by the poet Thomas Campion, who, speaking of Merlin in a masque of 1607, says, 'Prophet, tis true, and well we find the same, / Save only that thou didst mistake the name'),[2] who added the more historical evidence of their own descent from the Welsh prince Llewelyn (through the marriage of his daughter to Fleance, son of Banquo). But there was also a movement in the seventeenth century to stress the Saxon origin of England, in order to counter the royalist appropriation of Arthur. Anglo-Saxon history was the subject of much antiquarian research and writing, some of it taken up by parliament in order to oppose James I's insistence upon the divine right of kings by appealing to the witness of ancient Saxon laws. Throughout the century, the focus shifted from Briton to Saxon depending on which political party was in the ascendant. The pouring of scorn on the idea that the British nation originated with Brutus and on the claim for a historical Arthur are not simply the product of superior scholarship.

The edition of Malory that was published in 1634, the last for two centuries, is ambiguously related to this debate. It is a popular edition and has only one illustration, a woodcut depicting the Round Table. It is an unusual representation (though it is the way Layamon originally envisaged it), with the knights seated round the outside of the Table and King Arthur, in full armour, sticking out of a hole in the middle.[3] Though a round table with the centre cut out might in other circumstances provide a practical solution to the problems of table-service (especially with 1600 knights to feed), the picture here is undoubtedly peculiar. Does it assert the political centrality of the king (against the very idea of the Round Table), or does it make the idea of centrality ridiculous?

The political debates surrounding the English Civil War give a context also for Milton's allusions to Arthur. His comment on Arthur's historicity in his *History of Britain*, published in 1670 but written much earlier, is representative of the new attitude towards historical fact and the demand for hard evidence.

> But who *Arthur* was, and whether ever any such reign'd in *Britain*, hath bin doubted heertofore, and may again with good reason. . . . He who can accept of Legends for good story, may quickly swell a volume with trash, and had need be furnish'd with two only necessaries, leasure, and beleif, whether it be the writer, or he that shall read.

Yet Milton did propose at one time, as he says in one of his Latin poems, the *Epitaphium Damonis* (1640), to devote the epic poem that was to crown his poetic career to Arthur or some similar heroic-chivalric theme, something he chooses not to mention when he introduces Book IX of *Paradise Lost* with a call for inspiration in his high poetic endeavour, his 'Heroic Song', and a lofty scorn for older kinds of heroic poetry, declaring himself:

> Not sedulous by Nature to indite
> Wars, hitherto the only Argument
> Heroic deem'd, chief maistrie to dissect
> With long and tedious havoc fabl'd Knights
> In Battels feign'd.
> (IX.27–31)

In *Paradise Regained* the maidens who present the devil's tempting banquet to Christ in the wilderness are:

> Fairer than feign'd of old, or fabl'd since,
> Of Fairy Damsels met in Forest wide
> By Knights of Logres, or of Lyones,
> Lancelot, or Pelleas, or Pellenore.
> (II.358–61)

Milton's scorn of the Arthurian story has progressed, it will be seen, from doubt as to its veracity, through contempt for it as idle fiction, to the suggestion that it is akin to the devil's work. But is there a note of lingering nostalgic affection in his listings of names?

During the Commonwealth, Arthur almost disappears as a subject, but he had a revival with the Restoration. Dryden had plans for an Arthurian epic, but the only thing he did was the opera of *King Arthur*, with Purcell, designed to flatter Charles II but delayed in production until 1691, by which time there was a new and very different king on the throne and Dryden had to empty out all the politics and fill it up with fantasy and fairy tale (though this in itself was of course a political act).

> The final version, despite Dryden's laments, was fitted out with 'Beauties' enough to gain it immediate popularity; music by Purcell, dances by Priest, and such stage effects as a tree that gushes blood when struck by a sword, a fight between Arthur and Oswald [the Saxon leader] 'with Spunges in their hands dipt in blood', 'Syrens' who 'shew themselves to the Waste', and a forest scene which at the touch of a wand 'changes to a Prospect of Winter in Frozen Countries'.[4]

As Merriman comments, all the ingredients of a hit.

Sir Richard Blackmore, physician to William III, wrote two Arthurian epics, *Prince Arthur* (1695) and *King Arthur* (1697). The first tells an entirely new story of how Arthur has taken refuge on the continent after Uther's overthrow by the Saxons and now returns to England, with much angelic encouragement against diabolical intervention (in the manner of Homer), to fight and defeat the Saxons, who are much helped by Satan (in the manner of Milton) and marry a Saxon princess (in the manner of Virgil relating the story of Aeneas and Lavinia). The purpose is allegorically to represent King William, the hero of the Revolution of 1688, as the Christian warrior overcoming the pagan Saxons, that is, the Catholic Jacobites who supported James II and his son.

Arthur in the Eighteenth Century

Arthur sinks to the nadir of his fortunes in Henry Fielding's *The Tragedy of Tragedies*, or, *The Life and Death of Tom Thumb the Great* (1730), where Tom is a great hero at Arthur's court, despite being, as his name suggests, a midget. Arthur has a queen called Dollallolla, who is in love with Tom Thumb, and a daughter called Huncamunca, so in love with both Tom Thumb and the Lord Grizzle that she wants to marry them both. Arthur meanwhile is in love with Glumdalca, a captive giantess queen, who in her turn is in love with Tom Thumb. The dénouement comes when Tom Thumb, returning in triumph from defeating Lord Grizzle, is eaten by a cow. Everyone then kills everyone else, Arthur dying lastly by his own hand.

Fielding writes in burlesque parody of the high absurd style of contemporary tragic drama, and adds some further heavy irony at the expense of the learned scholars of Shakespearean drama with annotations by one Scriblerus Secundus. Arthur's opening lines give a good idea of the general tone:

> Let nothing but a face of joy appear.
> The man who frowns this day shall lose his head,
> That he may have no face to frown withal.
>
> (p. 357)

Arthur's name almost alone links the play with the tradition.

The eighteenth century was perhaps most likely of all to view Arthurian literature with contempt. Voltaire described the Middle Ages as 'a heap of crimes, follies, and misfortunes, sometimes in one country, sometimes in another, for five hundred years', while the Scottish philosopher David Hume regarded 'the interval between Augustus and the Renaissance as a great trough or depression, in which humanity wallowed for more than a thousand years a prey to ignorance, barbarism, and superstition'.[5] The eighteenth century needed of course to establish the existence of an age of barbarism in order to show off the new century as an age of enlightenment.

But with the renewal of interest in the natural against the artificial, of feeling against reason, of the ideal against the real, of the mysterious and evocative against the plain light of day, the medieval was bound to be seen differently. It was now needed for different purposes. The *Faerie Queene* was back in favour, and so was the art of chivalry, and then bardic poetry (in Ossian and Thomas Gray) and the 'ancient poetry' collected by Bishop Thomas Percy. It took longer for Arthur to regain literary status than the more generally medieval, associated as he was with children's and popular tastes, and when he did return, in the Romantic period, it was in a somewhat peculiar guise, not in the high Romantic medievalism of Coleridge's *Christabel* or of Keats's *Eve of St Agnes* and *La Belle Dame sans Merci* and 'charm'd magic casements opening on the foam / Of perilous seas in faery lands forlorn' but in the altogether more fashionable and glamorous concoctions of Sir Walter Scott. His work, both novels and poems, had an enormous influence on Victorian medievalism. It was a form of escapism, but like all escapism it served an important social purpose, for instance in allocating women an ideal yet non-operational role which anticipated that of the Victorian lady; in allowing men to share by proxy in the ideals of courtesy, service and self-denial which characterized their gentlemanly forefathers; and in detaching these particular kinds of art, culture and pleasure in them from the money-making activities that financed them. So a hard-nosed industrialist could build a Gothic mansion and fill it with medieval paintings and sculptures and stained glass, and thus withdraw it from all contact with the world of economic reality. Malory was reprinted, after two centuries, in 1816.

Sir Walter Scott

Scott promoted Arthurian medievalism with a pioneering edition (1804) of the medieval English romance of *Sir Tristrem*, which he claimed for Scotland, but his only original poem with a specifically Arthurian subject is *The Bridal of Triermain*. The romantic medievalism of Percy's *Reliques of Ancient English Poetry* (1765) had opened the way for the reromanticization of Arthur, and Scott duly took the hint. In *The Bridal of Triermain* a young swain Arthur recounts to Lucy, his beloved, an eerie vision of a beautiful woman that has appeared to Roland de Vaux, Lord of Triermain, and caused him to determine to find and marry her. Arthur's narration frames 'Lyulph's Tale', which explains the vision of the beautiful woman. It tells how King Arthur, out questing and not seeming to know particularly where he is going, comes to a castleful of beautiful maidens, under the charge of their beautiful queen, Guendolen. He loiters unforgivably (one of the pleasures of the medieval was the mild voyeurism that it seemed to license), with the consequence that Guendolen becomes pregnant, as she conveys to him with ineffable discreetness:

> . . . A moment mute she gazed,
> And then her looks to heaven she raised;
> One palm her temples veil'd, to hide
> The tear that sprung in spite of pride;
> The other for in instant press'd
> The foldings of her silken vest!
>
> (Canto 2, stanza III)

Arthur contrives to make his excuses, not as politely as he would like, and departs for Carlisle after escaping the very sticky end planned for him by Guendolen. Fifteen years of achievement follow (conquering Saxons, Romans, etc.) and then his daughter Gyneth arrives at court and demands to be jousted for, in accordance with Arthur's promise to her mother. The jousts are held, but she revels so excessively in men dying for her sake that Merlin (most recently in evidence as Tom Thumb's father) appears and condemns her to a sleeping state till she be awoken by a brave and noble and, as it turns out, very determined knight. We return now to the swain Arthur's story, which tells how Roland de Vaux, the Lord of Triermain, is always hanging around the castle where Gyneth lies asleep. He eventually gains entry, with much Gothic commotion of mysteriously appearing stairs, clanging portcullises, fierce beasts on guard, successive cavernous empty rooms, and of course battalions of fair and not so innocent damsels to distract him from his quest. It is a wonderful piece of medieval hokum, and it is not hard to see why it was so successful.

'The Return to Camelot'[6]

From the time of Sir Walter Scott, Arthurian chivalry was seen as the rather overstrained form of what made the modern system of manners. One of his great achievements was to bring chivalry up to date and make it acceptable as a model for his contemporaries. The enthusiasms were real, as in the life of Sir Kenelm Digby, who was always trying to create the circumstances of medieval Arthurian chivalry – holding tournaments, keeping vigil in King's College Chapel from dusk to dawn, rescuing a seventeen-year-old girl from 'a felon of the road' and escorting her home with all the gallantry of a knight-errant (no one is quite sure that she wanted to be rescued). His book,

The Broad Stone of Honour, had a great influence, as for instance on *Fraser's Magazine*, which not only fostered chivalric enthusiasms but also had its contributors eating and drinking and writing their copy at an Arthurian round table.

The Eglinton tournament of 1839 was perhaps inevitable. There had been a rather downbeat coronation in 1838, no banquet, no King's Champion riding into the banqueting hall, a marked shortage of chivalric flummery (whether due to economic recession or the pragmatic tastes of the prime minister, Lord Melbourne). There was opposition to this spirit of utilitarianism and commerce. There was also the opening of Samuel Pratt's armour showrooms in Lower Grosvenor Street in 1838. Pratt was as much the moving force behind the tournament as Lord Eglinton; he was in charge of all arrangements, and in addition to armour he was prepared to sell or hire crests, horse armour and equipment, pavilions, tents, shields, banners, lances, swords, outfits for squires and pages, and medieval costumes for the ball that was to take place on the evening of 28 August. It was to be held at Eglinton Castle in Ayrshire, 20 miles south of Glasgow, was to be open to the public as spectators, and the new rail connections made it possible for the public to get there in large numbers. All sorts of people applied to take part, with some asking if they could come in national dress or in a sailor's uniform or in Highland costume. To declare oneself a Conservative offered a better chance of being accepted.

Over 100,000 arrived; the procession, due to start at noon, did not appear; the sun went in; just after 3 p.m., when the procession was ready, and the Queen of Beauty installed in her carriage, there was a clap of thunder, and rain began to fall in torrents. It fell so for the rest of the day. Umbrellas went up, the procession squelched miserably through the puddles, the Queen of Beauty left in a closed carriage, the crowds drifted away. The tiltings were even worse; the knights slithered through the mud, rarely made contact; the covered grandstand started to leak in bucketfuls. When a halt was finally called, there were scenes of chaos as everyone tried to find a way through the mud to their carriages or to the nearest shelter. When the knights got up to the castle, they found that the marquee erected for the night's entertainments and ball had fallen down.

It was all remembered in a ludicrous fashion, especially by radical newspapers, with pictures of knights throwing down their lances and putting up umbrellas, but it is usually forgotten that on the following

Friday the sun came out, the tournament was held, with reasonable success – two of the participants, indeed, getting so carried away with the realism of it all that they lost their tempers and started laying into each other in real earnest – and the banquet and ball went off with great success.

Tennyson's *Idylls of the King*[7]

There were at least two Tennysons. The first was Alfred Tennyson, the shy and withdrawn son of a Lincolnshire clergyman who went up to Cambridge in 1828 at the age of nineteen as a budding poet and there developed a passionate friendship with Arthur Henry Hallam. Hallam died tragically in 1833; his death released in Tennyson a torrent of poetry of grief, longing, despair, lamentation, meditation on the futility of existence, mixed with sexual guilt and religious doubt, all commingled in his greatest poem, *In Memoriam* (published in 1850). The second Tennyson is the one who became poet laureate in 1850 (in succession to William Wordsworth), wrote a different kind of more public and 'responsible' poetry, became an icon of Victorian England, an idol of Queen Victoria, received a peerage in 1883 and died full of honours in 1892. His reputation, which was once as high as that of Shakespeare and Milton, underwent a steep decline in the 1920s, from which it has not fully recovered. From being the model of what a poet should be, he became a terrible warning of what a poet might become, of how the tormented anguish of the true poet might be embalmed in the conventional pieties of the establishment. *The Idylls of the King* belong firmly to the second half of his career, but they give evidence of the continuing conflict in Tennyson between the private world of sexual transgression and an imagined world of idealized public honour and perfected virtue.

Already in the 1830s, when there was a current of interest in Arthurian chivalry, Tennyson had dabbled with Arthurian legend, in 'Lancelot and Guenevere' (1830) and 'The Lady of Shalott' (1832), both with a strong erotic charge, and in the 'Morte d'Arthur' of 1842, written in some measure out of his continuing grief at the death of his own Arthur, Arthur Henry Hallam. But he was uneasy about the languorous seductiveness of the Arthurian 'dying fall', anxious that he ought to be more relevant, more positive, more attuned to the developing Victorian public morality. He enclosed the 'Morte d'Arthur' in a modern frame (a trick Scott had used to distance the author from his own indulgence in medievalism) which alludes to the idleness and irrelevance of such tales, and says that it is all that remains of the epic of Arthur in twelve books that he had written and then burnt because of his dissatisfaction with it. It is as if he anticipated the bad reviews that his twelve-book *Idylls* got forty years later and ingeniously had the whole work burnt before he had written it.

Tennyson took the Arthurian legend seriously, and was committed to a reworking of it, but in order to write an Arthurian cycle that was acceptable to Victorian public taste and to his own revised poetic persona, Tennyson had to take another tack. One idea was to concentrate on Galahad; another, which Tennyson eventually got round to, was to moralize the whole story into a fable of good and evil, soul and sense. But even in the 'Dedication to the Prince Consort', written just after Albert died in 1861, we can see how the attempt to create an ideal model of the perfect man (figuring Prince Albert), in whom sensuality was subdued to the higher virtues, or sense to soul, as he says in the epilogue 'To the Queen', was shadowed from the start. Arthur could not be that model for the Prince, because of course that would make Victoria into Guenevere, and Lancelot could not be the model, for obvious reasons; so when he described the Prince Consort,

> . . . And indeed He seems to me
> Scarce other than my king's ideal knight,
> 'Who reverenced his conscience as his king;
> Whose glory was, redressing human wrong;
> Who spake no slander, no, nor listen'd to it;
> Who loved one only and who clave to her –'
>
> (5–10)

where he originally had 'my own ideal knight' (which might be thought to refer to Arthur, or even Lancelot), he has to change it to 'my king's ideal knight', quoting lines from the evocation of the lost hope of the Round Table whose passing Arthur laments when he goes to berate Guenevere in the nunnery. They describe a non-existent hoped-for person who of course eventually arrived in the person of Prince Albert, the once and future Albert.

The twelve *Idylls* that follow are independent stories but they were arranged by Tennyson when he had completed them in a broadly chronological sequence, beginning with the 'Coming' and ending with the 'Passing' of Arthur and generally tracing the poisonous spread of the canker of Guenevere's adultery through the court and the realm. The process is of things generally getting much worse from never having been, except for a short time, very much better. This suits Tennyson pretty well. As to narrative technique, it is clear that Tennyson is doing what Vinaver said Malory did – disentangling the tellable tale – and perhaps this makes it clearer than it ever was that Malory wasn't exactly doing that. The twelve *Idylls* were published at intervals from 1859 to 1872, with 'Balin and Balan' (though written 1872–4) following in 1885. Malory is a source for only five of the twelve. They were arranged in the first full edition (1891) in the following order: 'The Coming of Arthur', 'Gareth and Lynette', 'The Marriage of Geraint', 'Geraint and Enid', 'Balin and Balan', 'Merlin and Vivien', 'Lancelot and Elaine', 'The Holy Grail', 'Pelleas and Ettarre', 'The Last Tournament', 'Guinevere' and 'The Passing of Arthur'. They are dealt with here in order of publication, except for 'The Coming of Arthur' and 'The Passing of Arthur'.

'The Coming of Arthur' (1869) shows many of the characteristic features of Tennyson's work on the Arthurian legend. There is first of all his inevitable tendency, given the age in which he lived, to explain things in rational and psychologically plausible terms. He explains, for instance, why Merlin carried off Arthur as soon as he was born – because the baby's life would be at risk from those who wished to seize Arthur's inheritance – and he leaves out the episode of the sword in the stone. The whole account of Arthur's birth is given in reply to Leodogran's enquiry into the parentage of a prospective son-in-law. Unlikely events are done as non-authorial narration, such as Queen Bellicent's story of a dragon-winged ship that appears in the heavens as a naked babe is delivered by a wave at Merlin's feet. There is also the desire to purge Arthur's career of doubts and ambiguities. So Ygerne is a 'stainless wife to Gorlois' who as to Uther 'so loathed the bright dishonour of his love' that she never voluntarily yields to him and is never compromised by the bed-trick; Uther is not transformed but just appears in his own person and forces her to 'wed him in her tears / And with a shameful suddenness'. Elsewhere no mention is made of Mordred's paternity: Arthur must be kept spotless, and must have no adventures with other women. Arthur's falling in love with Guenevere must be described in such a way as seemingly to exclude sexual attraction (which Tennyson tends to associate with illicit or adulterous or merely sensual love). Arthur is seen by Guenevere as he rides past, and he 'felt the light of her eyes into his life / Smite on the sudden'. It is almost like a mystical experience. But the real business of Arthur is cleansing the realm, an image which appears again and again in Tennyson, and is closely connected with the theme of sexual pollution. One of Tennyson's most powerful effects is to convey the closeness of wilderness and chaos, how easy it would be to revert to the bestial, of Arthur's court as a space of light in a surrounding and encroaching darkness. One of the vivid images is of the children seized by the she-wolf and 'housed / In her foul den . . . Till, straighten'd, they grew up to wolf-like men' – part of Tennyson's idea of the beast as that which threatens civilized community:

> And so there grew great tracts of wilderness,
> Wherein the beast was ever more and more,
> But man was less and less . . .
> (10–12)

It is this wilderness that Arthur cleanses:

> Then he drave
> The heathen; after, slew the beast, and fell'd
> The forest, letting in the sun, and made
> Broad pathways for the hunter and the knight
> And so return'd.
> (58–62)

At his coronation Arthur comes close to being a Christ-like figure, as Christ crucified in the stained-glass windows in the church shines down on him from three directions and all the order of the Round Table are transfigured into a 'momentary likeness of the King'.

Before 'The Coming of Arthur' there were four *Idylls* published in 1859 (called at the time 'Enid', 'Vivien', 'Elaine' and 'Guinevere'), all but one preoccupied with the threat to (male) society posed by (female) sexual promiscuity. 'Enid' tells the story we are familiar with from the *Erec et Enide* of Chrétien de Troyes, though Tennyson's actual source is the Welsh *Mabinogion*. It is a long poem, and Tennyson later split it into two, 'The Marriage of Geraint' and 'Geraint and Enid'.

From the start the impetus of the story derives from the obsessive theme and fear of sexual pollution. It is because of the 'rumour' of Guenevere's 'guilty love for Lancelot' (not of course the other way round) that Geraint withdraws himself and his wife from court, afraid that she may suffer or has already suffered 'some taint in nature' from her closeness to the queen. He returns to his own land, which is one of those border-lands of Arthur's realm, a prey to

> . . . bandit earls and caitiff knights,
> Assassins, and all flyers from the hand
> Of Justice, and whatever loathes a law. . . .
> . . . this common sewer of the realm
>   (35–9) –

the surrounding chaos that always threatens to engulf the shining city. But there his manhood sinks into 'mere uxoriousness', and Enid's sadness, which is simply concern at the way people are talking about him, he interprets as another sign that 'her nature had a taint' and that she is hankering after the court. One night in bed, thinking Geraint is asleep, she soliloquizes, lamenting his decline into 'mere effeminacy', fearing that it may in some obscure way be her fault and that she may not be 'a true wife'. Of course Geraint wakes up at this point, hears the last phrase, thinks all his fears are true, and flies into a rage. He tells Enid to get into her poorest clothes and be ready to go on quest. Then, prompted by the bringing out of the dress of faded silk that forms those poorest clothes, there follows the narrative, in flashback, of their courtship and marriage. The old dress is the one that Enid was wearing when Geraint first met her, and the one he insisted she wear when he brought her to Arthur's court. There is sentiment in this, but the old dress, and all its earlier history, play an important part in Tennyson's thinking. It seems that women must be stripped of all their fine array before it can be found out whether they have any truth in them. Men have an intrinsic moral being; women may have such a being, but only as it is reflected from men and if it is proved in them by men. Enid is only finally acceptable when she is proved, that is, to have no separate identity. This is a medieval idea – and a reminder of medieval stories of wife-testing such as Chaucer's Clerk's Tale – but it seems to have been acceptable also to Victorian gentlemen, and it is hard to believe that Tennyson took it over without being aware of what he was doing.

'Geraint and Enid' recurs to this theme, with Geraint lamenting that he wasted so much time tending his faithless wife, with care 'To dress her beautifully and keep her true' – as if her virtue were like a fragile vase entrusted to his keeping. The story of the testing, how he must prove her utterly, and go to irrational extremes to prove her truth, lacks the variety of tone and inventiveness of Chrétien. Geraint seems not an image of ruined nobility but a man in the grip of a dangerous neurosis. The beautifully extravagant unlikeliness of the old story, exposed now in a new psychological and dramatic realism, comes to seem like near-absurdity, as when, because Geraint is angry with her for telling him of the dangers that lie ahead on their path, against his express prohibition on her speaking a word, Enid resorts to sign-language to tell him of the next danger,

> At which the warrior in his obstinacy,
> Because she kept the letter of his word,
> Was in a manner pleased.
>
> (454–6)

The theme of cleansing is restated at the end when Arthur arrives to cleanse the border-lands. He speaks of the change that has taken place in Edyrn, Enid's wicked former suitor, since he was knocked on the head by Geraint:

> Full seldom doth a man repent, or use
> Both grace and will to pick the vicious quitch
> Of blood and custom wholly out of him,
> And make all clean, and plant himself afresh.
> Edyrn has done it, weeding all his heart
> As I will weed this land before I go.
>
> (901–6)

Emily Lady Tennyson's letter diary records at this time her husband's efforts to eradicate this vicious quitch-grass from his lawn at Farringford. Quitch-grass (or 'couch-grass'), with its deep and complex root structure, was evidently a torment to Tennyson comparable to ungovernable sexual desire.

'Merlin and Vivien' is cast in the form of a dialogue, with Merlin defending the high ideals of Arthur's court and Vivien arguing that purity is a denial and perversion of human nature – 'There is no being pure'. She is scornful of the notion that the love of Lancelot and Guenevere is anything but a sexual liaison – 'That glance of theirs, but for the street, had been / A clinging kiss'. It may be called 'a supersensual sensual love' but it's nothing but sex. She insinuates and slanders freely, and Merlin's arguments are undermined by his own reawakening sexual desires, his sense that this may be his last chance of flattering 'his own wish in age for love'. She also, in a twisted mirror-image of the story of Geraint and Enid, wants him to grant her his magical powers so that she will know that he is hers, because until then she cannot give herself to him fully – 'Yield my boon, / Till which I scarce can yield you all I am'. It is not a very subtle tactic, but it is an offer that Merlin finds it hard to refuse, though before being fondly overcome he speaks a last hopeless elo-quent praise of Arthur, 'blameless king and stainless man'. 'Man? is he man at all, who knows and winks?' says Vivien, which provokes Merlin to speak to himself, full of loathing for her but not wanting at this moment to ruin his chances:

> 'O true and tender! O my liege and King!
> O selfless man and stainless gentleman,
> Who wouldst against thine own eye-witness fain
> Have all men true and leal, all women pure.'
>   (789–92)

But women are where the whole plan breaks down:

> 'For men at most differ as Heaven and earth,
> But women, worst and best, as Heaven and Hell.'
>   (812–13)

It is a powerful poem, driven by Tennyson's own fears and fantas-ies and those of his age, as rendered in the famous picture of 'The Beguiling of Merlin' by Edward Burne-Jones, where Vivien has snakes in her hair (it is a Fall of Man) and a dress that, as Tennyson puts it, 'more exprest than hid her' (221).

'Lancelot and Elaine' is the most pleasing of all the *Idylls*, a wonder-ful retelling of Malory's story of the maid of Astolat. It begins with Tennyson's first full dramatic realization of the love-relationship of Lan-celot and Guenevere. They are in languid conversation, half arguing, half love-sick, and Lancelot wonders whether they shouldn't give it all up so that she can 'Henceforth be truer to your faultless lord'. She laughs scornfully,

> 'Arthur, my lord, Arthur, the faultless King,
> That passionate perfection, my good lord –
> But who can gaze upon the Sun in heaven?'
> (121–3)

As usual all the responsibility for the polluting nature of the relationship is placed upon the woman, but at least Tennyson gives her a chance to explain herself in a way that reminds one of Vivien but gives to the point of view a more sympathetic human colouring:

> 'He is all fault who hath no fault at all:
> For who loves me must have a touch of earth;
> The low sun makes the colour: I am yours,
> Not Arthur's, as ye know, save by the bond.'
> (132–5)

But the uniqueness of the poem is in the love of Elaine, whose selfless devotion to Lancelot Tennyson can write about with unmixed feelings. He evokes well the attraction that Lancelot's ravaged grandeur has for her when she first meets him:

> The great and guilty love he bare the Queen,
> In battle with the love he bare his lord,
> Had marr'd his face, and mark'd it ere his time.
> (244–6)

Tennyson touches on the irony of Arthur's hope that Lancelot's lonely heart may at least have found a love; and lingers affectionately on the thought, as Lancelot is recovering under her care from his wound, that if Lancelot had met her first,

> She might have made this and that other world
> Another world for the sick man; but now
> The shackles of an old love straiten'd him,
> His honour rooted in dishonour stood,
> And faith unfaithful kept him falsely true.
> (868–72)

Elaine's final revelation of her love, and Lancelot's bewildered but implacable response, make a dramatic scene, and her father's recommendation that Lancelot should be less courteous, should 'use some rough discourtesy / To blunt or break her passion', is echoed memorably in the scene of his departure:

> Then, when she heard his horse upon the stones,
> Unclasping flung the casement back, and look'd
> Down on his helm, from which her sleeve had gone.
> And Lancelot knew the little clinking sound;
> And she by tact of love was well aware
> That Lancelot knew that she was looking at him.
> And yet he glanced not up, nor waved his hand,
> Nor bad farewell, but sadly rode away.
> This was the one discourtesy that he used.
>
> (973–81)

After this the ending scenes of Lancelot's and Guenevere's recriminations and reconciliation seem quite petty.

'Guinevere' is again successful in giving a dramatic and human realization to the conflicts that elsewhere Tennyson has a tendency to moralize about more abstractly. She tells us, now in the nunnery, as the end draws near, that she was sick in spirit even before the last days of disaster and had called Lancelot to her chamber to tell him that they must finally part. So the meeting that Mordred and his creatures broke in upon was, ironically, their last. As she remembers these past events, the little nun-novice who is sitting with her (but does not know who she is) keeps babbling away about the wondrousness of the fellowship of the Round Table before it all fell apart because of the disloyal life of one woman. She talks of a kind of mystic oneness that existed between the land and the king before the queen came to spoil (and soil) everything. Guenevere is prompted to a hesitant defence of Lancelot and then, in a passage of touching beauty, to remember to herself their first meeting as Lancelot led her to Camelot to be married to Arthur, the development of their unspoken affection during the long journey, and how she finally met Arthur,

> . . . glanced at him, and thought him cold,
> High, self-contain'd, and passionless, not like him,
> Not like my Lancelot.
>
> (402–4)

In the midst of these broodings there arrives the king, en route to the last battle, come to denounce her finally. She hears the noise of the retinue arriving:

> . . . then came silence, then a voice,
> Monotonous and hollow like a Ghost's
> Denouncing judgment, but tho' changed, the King's.
>
> (416–18)

His speech is a terrible string of denunciations (Gladstone admired especially the 'awful severity' of Arthur's speech), what he had hoped for, how she had failed him, how it was all her fault, how she has been a disease, and how it is the worst fault in a man who knows his wife to be false not to expose her:

> For being thro' his cowardice allow'd
> Her station, taken everywhere for pure,
> She like a new disease, unknown to men,
> Creeps, no precaution used, among the crowd.
>
> (513–16)

Everything has gone wrong, 'And all thro' thee!' There is more of this self-righteousness ('I was ever a virgin save for thee') and, what's worse, 'vast pity' and forgiveness before Arthur's final gloomy

> 'Farewell!' And while she grovell'd at his feet,
> She felt the King's breath wander o'er her neck,
> And in the darknes o'er her fallen head,
> Perceived the waving of his hands that blest.
>
> (577–80)

That lack of touching, that 'waving', has more of the poet in it than any amount of sanctimonious speechifying from Arthur.

In 1869 Tennyson published 'The Holy Grail' and 'Pelleas and Ettarre', as well as 'The Coming of Arthur' and the revised form of 'The Passing of Arthur', and in 1871 'The Last Tournament'. They are for the most part dark reflections of a world grown old and corrupt, shot through with illusory gleams of brightness. The quest of 'The Holy Grail', told by Perceval in flashback form, bears the characteristic evidences of Tennyson's obsession in being motivated by the desire to cleanse the court of the stain of adultery. No mention is made of Galahad's paternity, a mark of Tennyson's determination to keep Lancelot pure of all sexual sin but with one. Arthur himself views the quest of the Grail as a distraction from the real work of cleansing the world – it is a retreat into a kind of private world that neglects the political duties that are placed upon kings and those who serve them. The quest itself is done with many poetic effects – Perceval in the desert of sand and thorns, Galahad fleeing across the endless bridge of fire, and Lancelot failing since all his virtues grow round one sin, 'until the wholesome flower / And poisonous grew together, each as each, / Not to be pluck'd asunder' (772–4).

'Pelleas and Ettarre' has a brilliant picture of Ettarre, a kind of Vivien-figure leading on the young Pelleas and then losing interest in him and getting exasperated with him and subjecting him to all sorts of humiliations, and then, ridiculously, loving him when he has learnt to despise her. Pelleas at first transforms his perception of Ettarre through the projection of his own innocence upon her (this seems to be true of much of Tennyson's portrayal of the way men love), but later transforms the whole world through the projection of Ettarre's corruption. He comes to Camelot, sees it as 'a black nest of rats', slanders Arthur to Perceval, meets Lancelot and challenges him with his adultery; Lancelot unhorses him dismissively and contemptuously, but refuses to kill him since Pelleas has no sword, and sends him to the queen.

> . . . The Queen
> Look'd hard upon her lover, he on her;
> And each foresaw the dolorous day to be:
> And all talk died, as in a grove all song
> Beneath the shadow of some bird of prey;
> Then a long silence came upon the hall,
> And Modred thought, 'The time is hard at hand'.
>   (591–7)

His world is constructed and then destroyed through a false imaging of female sexuality.

In 'The Last Tournament', Camelot is once more surrounded by the threat of the outer lands, the lawless and the heathen who dwell on the margins and threaten always to flood back, now under the leadership of the Red Knight of the North (Pelleas), who proclaims that his court is that of the anti-Round Table, full of harlotry and adultery but at least honest about it. Arthur rides north to subdue him, and does so, but in an orgy of massacre and destruction in which even his own knights are degraded. This is what happens also in the last tournament, the Tournament of the Dead Innocence, a travesty in which Lancelot takes Arthur's place as arbitrator but does nothing to see fair play (his own moral authority having been hollowed out from within by his sin), so that all sorts of rule-breakings are allowed. Even the weather is terrible. Significantly, the tournament is won by Tristram, whom Tennyson treats as an example of all that is most light and fickle in man's love. He is particularly pleased to win the prize ruby of the tournament because he wants something special to give to Isolt to smooth over her reaction to the news she is bound to have had of his marriage to Isolt of the White Hands, who functions as a mirror-image of Lancelot's Elaine. Tristram assures Isolt of Cornwall that he is not interested in the other Isolt –

> '... Isolt?
> Care not for her! patient and prayerful, meek,
> Pale-blooded, she will yield herself to God.'
> (601–3)

Most of the poem is a conversation between Tristram and Isolt of Cornwall, in which he is trying to persuade her that their love-affair is not over and if it seems in some ways deceitful then they have the example of Lancelot and Guenevere to go by, with the added incentive that there is no great shame in deceiving a wretched creature like Mark. But the shallowness of Tristram's love is betrayed when he says to Isolt, as he dallies with her hand, 'May God be with thee, sweet, when old and gray, / And past desire', which he may have intended as a harmless sentimentalism, but which throws Isolt into great perturbation. Where are your vows to love me for ever, she says; there was a time when the vows of a knight of Arthur meant something, but even if they mean nothing, even if you lie as you swear, yet,

> 'Swear to me thou wilt love me ev'n when old,
> Gray-hair'd, and past desire, and in despair.'
> (647–8)

Tristram says he will not swear any such thing; to do so would not be sensible, since it runs counter to the natural desires of the self (it might be Vivien speaking). There was a time when Arthur so dominated his court that he could instil in them for a while his own power of virtue,

> '. . . but then their vows –
> First mainly thro' that sullying of our Queen –
> Began to gall the knighthood, asking whence
> Had Arthur right to bind them to himself?'
>   (676–9)

What Arthur was trying to do was against nature. Is flesh and blood to be constrained thus?

> '. . . Can Arthur make me pure
> As any maiden child? . . .
> Bind me to one? The wide world laughs at it'.
>   (687–90)

It is the clearest statement of the theme of 'sense at war with soul' in the whole of the *Idylls*. Then at the end of the poem he gives the tournament ruby to Isolt:

> But, while he bow'd to kiss the jewell'd throat,
> Out of the dark, just as the lips had touch'd,
> Behind him rose a shadow and a shriek –
> 'Mark's way', said Mark, and clove him thro' the brain.
>   (745–8)

'Gareth and Lynette', published in 1872, was written quite late, when Tennyson realized he had given insufficient representation to the innocent early days of the Round Table. It is the longest of the *Idylls*, an enjoyable retelling of Malory's story, suitably rationalized and purged of its more bizarre sexual encounters. Tennyson does the repartee of Gareth and Lynette on the quest quite well, with nice touches of psychological observation, showing for instance how difficult it is for Lynette to overcome her first peevishness when she learns the truth about Gareth: she is pleased, but also annoyed that she has to be the last to find out. Gareth's explanation, when she expresses her amazement that he was so patient under her provocation – that he would not think much of any knight that let his heart 'Be stirred with any foolish heat / At any gentle damsel's waywardness' (1149–50) – might have been expected to provoke Lynette to hit him, but Tennyson probably thought it a polite enough retort. Tennyson deals with the complicated ending to Malory's story by leaving it out and simply having Gareth marry Lyonors straightaway – or as some say Lynette.

But Tennyson's main purpose in this idyll is to represent in Gareth all the highest idealism of the Round Table. Camelot is a kind of heaven to him, still completely untainted; all he is conscious of when he arrives are

> 'Eyes of pure women, wholesome stars of love,
> And all about a healthful people stept
> As in the presence of a gracious king'.
>
> (307–9)

It is the first age of Arthur, described in *Sir Gawain and the Green Knight*, before the shadow of adultery has fallen. Gareth himself is a kind of fanatical worshipper of Arthur and the Round Table; his image of himself is of an eagle swooping out of the Sun of Arthur to dash down all things base, 'working out his will / To cleanse the world'. His quest is not just a personal quest but part of a mission to destroy

> '. . . that old knight-errantry
> Who ride abroad, and do but what they will;
> Courteous or bestial from the moment, such
> As have nor law nor king.'
>
> (613–16)

One is reminded of old Hollywood westerns and the story they tell of the bringing under the law of the old breed of gunfighters.

'Balin and Balan', published in 1885, was the last of the *Idylls* to be written. Its story is of how slander destroys trust and eventually brings about the death of the two brothers at each other's hands, but the theme as always is the spreading taint of the adulterous love of Lancelot and Guenevere. The honest knight Balin is driven frantic by anguish and loathing at the hint of their impurity as he discovers it when eavesdropping upon their conversation in the garden. Lancelot speaks wistfully of his dream of a virgin saint with a 'spiritual lily' as the image of 'stainless maidenhood'. Guenevere sets against this the flowers that more symbolize the sensuality of sexual love:

> 'Sweeter to me,' she said, 'this garden rose
> Deep-hued and many-folded! sweeter still
> The wild-wood hyacinth and the bloom of May'.
>
> (264–6)

The implication is that, though men may have pure love in mind, women are sexual in their very being. It is this – the predatory nature of female sexuality – that seems to be what angers and terrifies Balin so much. Later Tennyson introduces Vivien to confirm Balin's worst fears. She enters singing a song of the old sun-worship which will return and destroy Arthur and his Round Table – 'The fire of Heaven is not the flame of Hell'. She is talking not so much about the destruction of Arthur's realm as about the resurgence of an irrational pagan sensuality, which is symbolized for Tennyson in the ungovernableness of female sexuality. Vivien, who wants to undermine Arthur and the Round Table and all that it stands for, gives a vividly erotic version of the scene that Balin eavesdropped on, which drives him into a wild frenzy, trampling in the dust the shield with Guenevere's crown on it that he has borne. Only in his dying moments does his brother Balan, who is like the other half of his tormented personality, tell him of Vivien and her followers:

> Foul are their lives; foul are their lips; they lied.
> Pure as our own true Mother is our Queen.
>
> (605–6)

This enables Balin to die happy, though deceived. Tennyson also introduces into this poem a kind of ultra-Arthur to show that he is aware of the absurdity of the extreme version of his position. King Pellam (who is a relic of the old Fisher King) rules a land from which women have been excluded:

> 'He boasts his life as purer than thine own;
> Eats scarce enow to keep his pulse abeat;
> Hath push'd aside his faithful wife, nor lets

Or dame or damsel enter at his gates
Lest he should be polluted.'
(101–5)

Tennyson, engaged in trying to channel the mysterious and dangerous powers of female sexuality, seems to recognize the passionless sterility which results from damming up that power. Tennyson's Arthurian cycle as a whole is interestingly related to the effort of nineteenth-century male writers to respond to and contain the growing clamour of women's voices to be heard, which they construed (not for the first nor the last time) as the threat of sexual domination and promiscuity.

The short poem of 'The Passing of Arthur', which first appeared in 1842, was published in revised form in 1869. Arthur is continuing (after 'Guinevere') on his way to the last battle, and cries out as he sees his land reverting to savagery:

'. . . and all my realm
Reels back into the beast, and is no more.
My God, thou hast forgotten me in my death:
Nay – God my Christ – I pass but shall not die.'
(25–8)

The echo of Christ's words on the Cross is explicit, as is the faith in the hope of resurrection, neither perhaps very appropriate. There follows the marvellous description of the last battle, 'this last, dim, weird battle of the west', fought in a mist that cloaks all. The 1842 poem, with its account of Bedivere and the casting of Excalibur into the mere (the finest descriptive poetry in all the *Idylls*), is picked up at line 170 and carries to 440, after which Tennyson adds the final lines in which Bedivere goes to a higher point on the cliff and sees the boat disappearing in the distance and hears a great cry as of a city greeting its king who has been long away on his wars, and saw,

Or thought he saw, the speck that bare the King,
Down that long water opening on the deep
Somewhere far off, pass on and on, and go
From less to less and vanish into light.
And the new sun rose bringing the new year.
(465–9)

The dedication 'To the Queen' was written in 1872, when all but 'Balin and Balan' were written. It is a chance for Tennyson to declare his theme again, and detach his Arthur, as an allegorical ideal, from the misty king of legend or quasi-history. He asks the queen to accept

> . . . this old imperfect tale,
> New-old, and shadowing Sense at war with Soul,
> Ideal manhood closed in real man,
> Rather than that gray king, whose name, a ghost,
> Streams like a cloud, man-shaped, from mountain peak,
> And cleaves to cairn and cromlech still . . .
>
> (36–41)

Tennyson's poem was immensely popular with his readers, but had a mixed reception from the critics, who admired the language and picturesque description but charged Tennyson with fleeing from real life and the horrors of the industrial revolution behind a medieval arras. Tennyson maintained against this that his Arthurian cycle did have a point, that it did deal with major issues of the time – the corruption of society and the individual that results from neglect of moral and spiritual values – and did this by depicting the struggle of sense (Guenevere) and soul (Arthur) for what is most admirable in man (Lancelot). Tennyson was quite flattered to find his poem being taken seriously and allegorized, though anxious that it should not be tied down to reductively abstract interpretations. In himself he knew that the critics (like Carlyle) who demanded social relevance were wrong, and that that part of himself that demanded it was his least poetic part. His great power lay in the dramatic and human realization of love and love's decay, and above all in that great threnody upon the lost past that instils its mourning into all his poetry.

Victorian Arthurianism

Tennyson was not alone in returning to the Arthurian legend for inspiration. Matthew Arnold's *Tristram and Yseult* (1852) tells of Tristram's last meeting with Yseult when he is dying, and ends with the memories of Iseult of Brittany. After extracting every ounce of languorous romantic love-yearning from the story, Arnold, all passion spent, turns rather petulantly on romantic passion – 'Being, in truth, but a diseas'd unrest, / And an unnatural overheat at best'. Algernon Charles Swinburne's *Tristram of Lyonesse*, perhaps his major poem, is by contrast unashamedly romantic. The style is hypnotically alluring, and at least a cure for insomniacs. William Morris also used Arthurian episodes in his narrative poems.

In some respects, Arthur was a problem for late Victorian readers. So much had to be obscured or only hinted at. In the retellings of Malory for younger people, beginning with J. T. Knowles's *The Story of King Arthur* in 1862, there was an attempt to paint out whatever was 'so crude in taste and morals as to seem unworthy of the really high-minded author of 500 years ago'.[8] Lancelot was a particular problem, and so he was made to worship the queen from afar, or else it was just a mysterious 'treason' that Lancelot and Guenevere were guilty of, adultery remaining unmentioned, or else the accusations were mentioned but condemned as false and as the product of the others' envy. This was the version recommended by Baden-Powell to his Boy Scouts in 1908. He, incidentally, was much influenced by the Knights of King Arthur founded in 1893 by a Congregational minister from Vermont called William Byron Forbush. Its members (led by adult Merlins) met round a Round Table, took the names of knights and transformed their games and outings into Arthurian quests and battles. The retellings of Malory, with the roles of Lancelot and Guenevere sponged clean, contributed to another fantasy Indian summer of Arthurian chivalry. There was a consequence to this, as Girouard argues: the ideals of chivalry worked to glorify war, in so far as it was associated with the paraphernalia of chivalry, and to encourage 2.5 million men to volunteer for the army in 1914. Chivalry sank in the mud of Flanders, like a nightmare parody of the Eglinton tournament, or a nightmare fulfilment of Mark Twain's apocalyptic vision.

The Pre-Raphaelites took a different approach: they were well prepared to paint scenes of sexual suggestiveness, and Burne-Jones was particularly fascinated (and appalled) by the story of Merlin and Vivien. He did five pictures of the sage-wizard and his demon-mistress, including the famous 'Beguiling of Merlin' (1875–7) now in the Lever Art Gallery in Port Sunlight. His masterpiece is perhaps 'The Sleep of Arthur in Avalon' (1880–98, unfinished) in Puerto Rico.

In addition to panel painting, there was much Arthurian book illustration. Dante Gabriel Rossetti did three of the six illustrations in the

Moxon Tennyson of 1857, and Gustave Doré illustrated the four *Idylls* that came out in 1859. Julia Margaret Cameron provided photographic illustrations, at Tennyson's request, for the *Idylls* of 1875. She was an innovative photographic artist, and she staged scenes with real-life models: the lady chosen to be Vivien declared that at first 'I very much objected, because Vivien did not seem to me to be a very nice person'. Aubrey Beardsley did 500 illustrations for the *Morte D'Arthur* brought out by Dent in 1893–4 in imitation of the Kelmscott Press editions. Beardsley characteristically treats the knights as passive, androgynous figures, reclining or sleeping in compositions dominated by women. There is also much Victorian or Victorian-inspired Arthurian stained glass and mural-painting, including the Malory windows in Princeton University Chapel, the Dunlop windows done by William Morris and friends now in the Bradford City Art Gallery, and the mural paintings of the Grail story by Edwin Austin Abbey in the Boston Public Library.

7

Mark Twain, T. H. White, John Steinbeck and the Modern Arthur

Mark Twain, *A Connecticut Yankee in King Arthur's Court*

How seriously the Arthurian story was coming to be taken as a parable for the instruction of a decadent age is well illustrated in Mark Twain's *A Connecticut Yankee in King Arthur's Court* (begun in 1886, a year after the publication of Tennyson's 'Balin and Balan', and completed in 1890), where Twain's determination to provide a comic spoof of Arthurianism is gradually eroded by his own recognition that the ridiculous world of chivalry had an idealism and humanity that the modern world of commerce and profit has destroyed. The destruction wrought by the Yankee on Arthurian England at the end, not just on the knights of the Round Table but also on his own factories and workshops and schools and newspaper offices, is Twain's revenge on the world that has rejected and defeated his determination to improve it. It is in many ways a disturbing work, not the product of a grand satirical design but of a mind that switches uncontrollably between naive idealistic hope of change and reform, on the one hand, and homicidal irritation at people for not wanting to be changed and reformed in the way he proposes.

Though Hank Morgan is not to be simply identified with Twain, the book follows closely the reactions of its author to what was happening in the world, in the American south, in South and Central America, and, as he heard from the lectures of George Kennan, in the Siberian slave-labour camps, the gulags of the Tsarist empire. Twain's response to these revelations of the systematic cruel dehumanizing of human beings by their fellow creatures was the cry of despair, almost deranged, that one hears also at the end of *A Connecticut Yankee*: 'If such a government cannot be overthrown otherwise than by dynamite,' he said of the Tsarist regime, after one of Kennan's lectures, 'then thank God for dynamite.' Dynamite, machine guns, electrified barbed wire, minefields, are the instruments of Twain's anger at the end of *A Connecticut Yankee*, anger at England, at America, at the human race, and of course at himself.

In the framing narrative, Twain meets with a mysterious stranger as he is being shown round Warwick Castle, and acquires from him an old book, written on parchment; he spends all night reading it, but when he goes back in the morning to return it to the stranger, he finds him dying, and soon dead. This is one of those devices for distancing the narrative from the author by claiming an authoritative text as intermediary, and is widely used by authors, with different degrees of intention of being taken seriously, from Geoffrey of Monmouth, with his old Welsh book, to Umberto Eco, in *The Name of the Rose*. The manuscript he reads is the story of the stranger, Hank Morgan, an enterprising and self-confident factory superintendent from Hartford who is laid out cold 'during a misunderstanding conducted with crowbars with a fellow we used to call Hercules' in the factory where he works (p. 5). He is projected back to the year 529, where he sets about reforming Arthurian society until at the end Merlin, otherwise a hopeless old fuddy-duddy, always casting spells that don't work, manages to put a spell on him that sends him back to where he belongs.

Within this 'envelope', the narrative tells how the Yankee is captured by Sir Kay, taken to Camelot, befriended by the young squire Clarence, and put in prison, but wins power by causing, as it appears, an eclipse of the sun as a display of his annoyance. He demonstrates his power further – since, as he says, a magician has to work a few miracles to keep up his reputation – by blowing up Merlin's tower (a handsome old stone tower, 'after a rude fashion', he remarks, in passing, p. 56), and then proceeds with his plans for reform. Soon he feels obliged to undertake a quest – knights, even the Boss, as he is now called (with somewhat sinister echoes both of the 'boss' of the southern plantations and the boss of northern machine-politics), have to go out on adventures – and he takes up the cause of the lady Alisaundre, whom he calls Sandy. In the course of the quest they visit Morgan le Fay's castle, its dungeons and torture chambers full of monstrous evidences of the cruelty and inhumanity of the old regime, meet with pilgrims and slaves, and at the pilgrimage-shrine the Boss performs the miracle of the Fountain, where fireworks are used to make a great display of magical power after a leak in the well-spring has been simply repaired by other means. The return to Camelot sees the introduction of more innovations, including competitive examinations for government officials, and newspapers, and then the Boss goes out again on adventures, this time with the king incognito, so that he may learn something of the condition of his people. They are taken as slaves and eventually rescued by Lancelot, after which follows the fight with the unreformed knights of the Round Table, in which cowboy lariats and revolvers prove more successful than swords and lances. Three years pass, and the reform of England into a modern technocratic state continues until, after a short absence from the country, the Boss returns to find it under interdict and fallen back into its old bad ways. There follow the last battle, and Twain's own final battle, the Battle of the Sandbelt.

Twain began the book as a light-hearted and wisecracking take-off of Arthurianism, with much fun derived from the confrontation between the aggressively entrepreneurial Yankee with his technical know-how and the antique maundering ways of old England. The light-heartedness gradually evaporates, and the book becomes a savage attack on feudalism and religion and all that holds man in thrall to sentiment and irrational tradition. Twain was writing for amusement but found himself using the story of Arthur in the way we have constantly seen it being used – as a vehicle for new ideas and ideals about how society might be run. It is a measure of the resilience of the ancient story that it resists some of these pressures towards appropriation, exerts its own evocative powers, and reveals in the process something of the hollowness of pragmatic utilitarianism.

The most enjoyably Arthurian parts of *A Connecticut Yankee* are the specific allusions to Arthurian legend, and the comical way they are managed, for instance the first mention of the love of Lancelot and Guenevere, when the queen receives the prisoners at Lancelot's hands:

> Well it was touching to see the queen blush and smile, and look embarrassed and happy, and fling furtive glances at Sir Launcelot that would have got him shot in Arkansas, to a dead certainty. (p. 24)

In allusion to the traditional Arthurian motif where knights defeated on a quest are told to go to Camelot and yield themselves to the king, here the Boss sends likely men to Camelot with instructions to report to Clarence and be 'put in the manufactory' of good men or 'man-factory' (p. 114). There's also a reprise of a favourite episode – Lancelot's arriving in the nick of time to rescue Guenevere from the flames – with Lancelot and five hundred mailed and belted knights arriving on bicycles, this time to rescue Arthur just as he is about to be hanged as a slave (p. 379).

Twain is specially fascinated by the language of the Arthurian story as it is told by Malory. There are long verbatim quotations from Malory early in the book, and Sandy passes the time when they are on quest by telling long stories taken straight from Malory. On one occasion the Yankee falls asleep in the midst of her recital and wakes up to find her still steaming steadily on; he has missed a chapter, but it doesn't make a lot of difference. As he says to Sandy, the descriptions are too monotonous, 'run too much to level Saharas of fact, and not enough to picturesque detail' (p. 130):

> A couple of people come together with great random, and a spear is brast, and one party brake his shield, the other one goes down, horse and man, and brake his neck, and then the next candidate comes randoming in . . . (p. 131)

Twain goes on thus for a page or so. Another comment is on the lack of differentiation in Malory's use of dialogue. When the Irish knight Sir Marhaus comes in, the Yankee tells Sandy that it is not good form that he should speak like all the rest; he should be given a brogue, or at least 'a characteristic expletive', like 'be jabers'. 'It is a common literary device with the great authors', he says (p. 133). Twain is also a wonderful satiric mimic of Malory's style, as when the Yankee tries to get Sandy to say what direction they are to take to get to the castle:

> 'Ah, please you, sir, it hath no direction from here, by reason that the road lieth not straight, but turneth evermore; wherefore the direction of its place abideth not, but is sometime under the one sky and anon under another . . .' (p. 92)

And so on, interminably. Sandy later complains that she cannot al-ways understand what the Boss says, telling him this in a huge, long, almost unintelligible and hilariously plausible sentence (p. 212) – an extraordinary *tour de force*.

We also enjoy, particularly in the earlier, more light-hearted part of the book, the comedy of out-of-placeness, the absurdity of romance-conventions as they are seen by a modern practical person, like the Yankee's first meeting with an armed knight: ' "Fair sir, will ye joust?" said this fellow. "Will I which?" "Will ye try a passage of arms for land or lady or for –" "What are you giving me?" I said. "Get along back to your circus or I'll report you" ' (p. 5). Twain draws much amusement from the narrative realization of some of the unrealized fantasy of romance – what it was like to spend any time actually in armour, in chapter 12, 'Slow Torture' (what we admired the poet of *Sir Gawain and the Green Knight* for touching on, even lightly, is here made systematically ridiculous), or the convention that knights on quest never had to stop for food (p. 107).

The Yankee himself begins as the practical Connecticut man who has a knowledge of engineering and how to fix things, but he soon reveals a less attractive side to his character:

> I made up my mind to two things: if it was still the nineteenth century and I was among lunatics and couldn't get away I would presently boss that asylum or know the reason why; and if on the other hand it was really the sixth century, all right . . . I would boss the whole country inside of three months. (p. 17)

There is much more of this: when the miracle of the Fountain is accomplished the people fall back reverently 'to make a wide way for me, as if I had been some kind of a superior being – and I was. I was aware of that' (p. 224). The Yankee carries in himself both the efficiency and the inhumanity of the new machine age. He thinks of himself as a new Joseph serving a British Pharaoh, but his contempt for those he serves is constantly expressed – there was no competition, he says, 'not a man who wasn't a baby to me in acquirements and capacities' (p. 63). Twain introduces distortions in the viewpoint of the narrator so that he can overdo the satire in an extravagant and comically ridiculous way without making us think that it is the author who has taken leave of his senses – a little like Gulliver in Swift's *Gulliver's Travels*.

Yet Twain is so personally involved in what he writes about that he cannot maintain the distance that is necessary for his narrator; he

hates what he hates so much that the viewpoint (maybe not unlike
that of Gulliver) is not objectively controlled but skewed. So he shifts
like a weathervane between his love of people as they are for what
they are and his detestation and contempt for them for what they are
not. He is touched by their innocent simplicity, but angered by their
habit of passive resignation, the demeanour for instance of the other
prisoners in Arthur's court, 'their faces, their clothing, caked with
black and stiffened drenchings of blood' (p. 20), who utter no groan
or cry of complaint. At first he thinks it an admirable kind of philo-
sophical fortitude, but then he realizes it is mere animal training:
'they are white Indians' (p. 20). He finds in them a 'fine manliness',
'a certain loftiness and sweetness that rebuked your belittling criti-
cisms' (p. 23), but it is as if he has to keep guarding himself from this
weakness by treating them as children. 'It was just like so many
children', he says, of the laughter provoked by Dinadan's japes and
funny stories (p. 30).

The fascinating and disturbing reversal within the book is that this
childlikeness comes to seem irresistibly attractive, as we see more and
more what actually constitutes this 'superior being', for instance his
unbounded delight when he enters the lists as the 'champion of hard,
unsentimental, common-sense and reason' (p. 355) against old knight-
errantry, and smashes all-comers with his lariat and finally his revolvers: 'I sat there drunk with glory' (p. 389), 'I never did feel so happy
as I did when my ninth shot downed its man' (p. 393).

> The day was mine. Knight-errantry was doomed. The march of civil-
> ization was begun. How did I feel? Ah, you never could imagine it.
> (p. 393)

He cannot imagine a greater delight than outsmarting people and
pulling off effects; smart explanations are his forte, as they are with
Brer Rabbit and Huckleberry Finn, two of his ancestors. When Sandy
tells him tenderly that she has named their child (whose appearance
is a great surprise in a book that has no sex at all) 'Hello-Central'
(because that is what Hank keeps murmuring fondly in his sleep,
reminding himself of his Connecticut girlfriend, a telephone oper-
ator), he is not so much touched as in danger of rupturing himself
by bursting out laughing, but pleased that he is smart enough not to
burst out laughing, and pleased too to have a smart answer when she

finds out that every telephone call in the country begins with the name of their child. He seems to lack, or rather to suppress, that capacity to feel shame that I described, in talking about *Sir Gawain and the Green Knight*, as being so important to civilized behaviour, and which is so much the quality of those he mocks; he lacks the very quality that chivalry nurtured. Twain seems partly to realize all this, since he ends his postscript with an allusion to the Yankee's fondness for 'effects': 'He was getting up his last "effect"; but he never finished it' (p. 447).

But there is a deeper level to the disturbance within the work that is not to do with the unsettling quality of the narrative voice. There is a sentimentality in the attachment to certain persons or qualities, but a great readiness to see people in the mass as merging into an inanimate solid chunk of matter, easy to obliterate from mind. The Yankee is very fond of referring to crowds of people that he is impressing with his effects as 'acres of human beings' (p. 59); '250 acres of people' (p. 219) come to watch the miracle of the Fountain, 'you could have walked upon a pavement of human heads to – well, miles' (p. 221). A particular variation is to blur the line between the animate and the inanimate – the source also of much of Twain's most characteristic humour, incidentally – as when he describes the effect of the dynamite bomb he throws at the advancing knights:

> Yes, it was a neat thing, very neat and pretty to see. It resembled a steamboat explosion on the Mississippi; and during the next fifteen minutes we stood under a steady drizzle of microscopic fragments of knights and hardware and horse-flesh. (p. 272)

The 'effect' is the same in the blowing up of the minefield in the Battle of the Sandbelt:

> Of course, we could not count the dead, because they did not exist as individuals, but merely as homogeneous protoplasm, with alloys of iron and buttons. (p. 432)

At the end of the narrative of this battle, the Yankee is berserk, in a kind of homicidal tantrum, like the maniac general played by George C. Scott in Stanley Kubrick's film of *Dr Strangelove*: 'I shot the current through all the fences and struck the whole host dead in their tracks! *There* was a groan you could *hear*!' (p. 440).

It takes no ingenuity to see in this readiness to treat people as a mass, to be shaped to the will of a superior being or else to be destroyed, the lineaments of what later came to be called fascism. The acres of people, like a pavement of human heads, are what Hitler saw and glorified in his power over at the Nuremburg rallies. The knights that the Boss sends round the country selling soap and toothpaste – a good way of making use of the habits of knight-errantry – are quite comical, but not so comical is the other system that he develops:

> I had had confidential agents trickling through the country some time, whose office was to undermine knighthood by imperceptible degrees, and to gnaw a little at this and that and the other superstition, and so prepare the way gradually for a better order of things. (p. 83)

One of his deepest secrets is his military academy, and another the naval academy he has established at a remote seaport, both of which he keeps most jealously out of sight. He cannot tell people about these things, because if he did tell them they wouldn't want them, and that would be because they are stupid. This of course is the argument of all totalitarian governments. We do what we do for the good of the people, because they are not smart enough to know for themselves what is good for them. They are just children.

Beyond this lies a profound uncertainty in Twain about what he thinks of people as social beings. He has a series of tirades against monarchy, aristocracy and the Catholic church, including a wonderfully incendiary account of feudalism (ch. 13), brimming with outrage. Against the horrors of feudal aristocracy and the rule of privilege, he sets the example of American democracy, arguing that 'a privileged class, an aristocracy, is but a band of slaveholders under another name' (p. 239). The slaveholder's blunted feeling towards his fellow-creatures is the same as that of the aristocrat, and 'the result of the same cause in both cases: the possessor's old and inbred custom of regarding himself as a superior being' (p. 239 – the Yankee seems to have forgotten that this is what he claimed to be).

As long as he is engaged in these tirades, Twain is irresistible, for he has the torrential eloquence of the born orator. When he tries to use narrative to support his arguments he is less successful, and some of the least effective episodes are those where he tries to whip up social indignation and create revulsion at the enormity of the outrages committed in the name of feudalism – the racking of the young husband in front of his wife in Morgan le Fay's castle (ch. 17) or the burning at the stake of a young mother and her child (ch. 35). It is a cheat: Twain manufactures these episodes out of the most tawdry material (usually involving children and young and beautiful distressed maidens) to fuel his indignation, but the effect is wholly contrived.

The ultimate ineffectualness of these passages is rooted in a deep conflict in Twain about people. Are they intrinsically good, or are they mere inert material to be shaped by superior beings? It is the question asked not by tyrants but by those who despair of democracy. At times Twain will insist that people are infinitely malleable:

> Training – training is everything; training is all there is to a person. We speak of nature; it is folly; there is no such thing as nature; what we call by that misleading name is merely heredity and training. (p. 162)

On another occasion it is not training that he calls it but the indoctrination of experience: when the pilgrims meet the band of slaves and watch the flogging of the young mother, they only comment on the expert way with which the whip is used:

> They were too much hardened by life-long every-day familiarity with slavery to notice that there was anything else in the exhibition that invited comment. This was what slavery could do, in the way of ossifying what one may call the superior lobe of human feeling. (p. 200)

It makes Twain despair (and we must talk of Twain here, not the Yankee) – this 'monotonous dead level of patience, resignation, dumb uncomplaining acceptance' (p. 182) – and convinces him that nothing will ever be changed by 'goody-goody talk', 'it being an immutable law that all revolutions that succeed must *begin* in blood, whatever may answer afterward' (p. 183).

Against this has to be put that phrase, 'the superior lobe of human feeling', which implies some instinctive inner quality, the other pole that Twain sways to in his confusion and uncertainty. He constantly recognizes inherent goodness in people, despite the lives of indoctrination that should have turned them into zombies. The king himself is the focus of much of the Boss's anger and frustration and grudging awareness of something in human beings that lies beyond the power of both training (in the good sense) and servile indoctrination (in the bad sense). There is great comedy in the chapter called 'Drilling the King' (ch. 28), where he is trying to get the king to behave like an ordinary person, but later he realizes that what he is trying to drill out of the king is precisely what the worthwhileness of his identity is grounded in. The episode in 'The Small-Pox Hut' (ch. 29) is extravagantly overdone, like all Twain's sentimental passages, but it certainly presents an alternative to utilitarianism. Arthur cannot be persuaded against going to fetch the dying child (another slender girl of fifteen, incidentally) downstairs to be with her dying mother:

> Here was heroism at its last and loftiest possibility, its utmost summit; this was challenging death in the open field unarmed, with all the odds against the challenger, no reward set upon the contest, and no admiring world . . . to applaud; and yet the king's bearing was as serenely brave as it had always been in those cheaper contests. . . . He was great, now; sublimely great. (pp. 285–6)

But a few pages later, when Arthur goes out chasing the miscreants who have set fire, in a laudably revolutionary way, to the manor-house of the wicked lord, Twain is once more in exasperation:

> There it was, again. He could see only one side of it. He was born so, educated so, his veins were full of ancestral blood that was rotten with this sort of unconscious brutality, brought down by inheritance from a long procession of hearts that had each done its share towards poisoning the stream. (p. 292)

It is as if Twain wants people to be intrinsically good, and suitable to have the vote in a democratic community, and then he cannot contain his anger when they fall short, and he just wants to smash them or shoot them or blow them up with dynamite. It is not what one would call a deep faith in the democratic process (and in its more horrific and diseased form it will lead to the Oklahoma bombing).

At the end, in 'Three Years Later' (ch. 40), Twain tries to recapture some of the zest and comic spirit of the earlier part of the book, putting all the earls and barons to work on the railway trains, casually hanging the compiler of a book of bad jokes, sending out knights as sales representatives, getting ready an expedition to discover America, destroying the Catholic church and setting up a republic. But the church hits back. 'Did you think you had educated the superstition out of this people?' asks Clarence (p. 418). No: it was the priests who sent him cruising with his family, got him out of the country so that they could re-establish their power over the people:

> The Church, the nobles and the gentry turned one grand, all-disapproving frown upon the people and shrivelled them into sheep! (p. 427)

There is only one way with this 'human muck' (p. 427), and in the alarming last pages of the book Twain turns his full power as a writer to a murderously gleeful vision of extermination, the electrified fences, trenches and machine guns on fixed lines of fire of the Battle of the Sandbelt so graphically anticipating in the killing-fields of fiction the horrors of trench-warfare of the 1914–18 war.

Twain's great book should not be left there without recognizing again the cracker-barrel brilliance of the writing and his inventiveness with that kind of metaphor that runs animate and inanimate into one, amidst ridiculous collapsings of scale, like this little riff on the smallness of Britain's kingdoms:

> 'Kings' and 'Kingdoms' were as thick in Britain as they had been in little Palestine in Joshua's day, when people had to sleep with their knees pulled up because they couldn't stretch out without a passport. (p. 141)

Or the image he uses for Arthur as he gets up very slowly to do his imitation of an ordinary person:

> 'True, I had forgot it, so lost was I in planning of a huge war with Gaul' – he was up by this time, but a farm could have got up quicker, if there was any kind of a boom in real estate. (p. 265)

Perhaps most characteristic of all is Twain's way of materializing language in extraordinary forms, like the newspaper extracts, perhaps his favourite moment of indulgence in the whole book (ch. 26), or the scene in the castle of Morgan le Fay when she slips a dirk into the young boy who trips against her:

> Poor child, he slumped to the floor, twisted his silken limbs in one great straining contortion of pain, and was dead. Out of the old king was

wrung an involuntary 'O-h!' of compassion. The look he got from the queen made him cut it suddenly short and not put any more hyphens in it. (p. 144)

Is this the inspiration of the unfinished inscription ('The castle of Aaaaagggh . . .') on the wall of the cave guarded by the monster rabbit in the film of *Monty Python and the Holy Grail*?

The illustrations to *A Connecticut Yankee* by Daniel Beard are not the least of its pleasures. Twain said in December 1889 that Beard 'had illustrated the book throughout without requiring or needing anybody's suggestions, and to my mind the illustrations are better than the book – which is a good deal for me to say, I reckon'.

T. H. White, *The Once and Future King*

It was to the service of another form of naive social idealism that the story of Arthur was pressed in the cycle of Arthurian novels of T. H. White, *The Once and Future King*. Enormously successful – and not only as a children's book – White's version of Malory's events is also made into a commentary on the politics of the 1930s, in which White's hatred of popular democracy is inscribed in the narration almost as violently as his hatred of totalitarianism.

The Sword in the Stone was published in 1938, *The Queen of Air and Darkness* in 1939 and *The Ill-Made Knight* in 1940. These three books stood as a trilogy until the publication of *The Candle in the Wind* in 1958, when the four books were put out together as *The Once and Future King*. *The Book of Merlyn*, written 1941, but not published until 1977, is the book in which White, who had always found fascination in animals, finally decides that he prefers them to people. *The Once and Future King* is a boy's book, or a young person's book, but the author often addresses an adult audience over their heads (in an insufferably knowing way).

The first book, *The Sword in the Stone* (the best and most original of the four), deals with the education of Arthur, called Wart, by his tutor Merlyn, while he lives in the castle of his foster-father, old Sir Ector, and Ector's son Kay. Much of Wart's education is through being turned into animals – a fish, a merlin ('very good choice', says Merlyn, p. 76), an ant, a wild goose and a badger (p. 184) – so that he

can learn what being in a different element is like and gain an intuit-
ive understanding of his own world (a variant of Twain's idea that
the king should have experience of what it is like to be an ordinary
man). Wart's education is interspersed with the comic episodes of
King Pellinore and his pursuit of the Questing Beast, and there is also
the visit to Robin Wood in Sherwood Forest, and the night-attack on
the castle of Morgan le Fay, made entirely of food (except for Morgan
le Fay), where she rests on a bed of lard, guarded by a griffin. The
book ends with the sword in the stone and the coronation, with all
the animals present to give Arthur the power that derives from their
love (a little reminiscent of the theme of the mystical union of the
king and his land introduced by Tennyson in 'Guinevere').

The second book, *The Queen of Air and Darkness*, is about the first
great battle, the battle of Bedegraine, and how Arthur learns the
painful lesson that there has to be bloody fighting before he can set
up his new order. The battle is counterpointed against a series of
scenes in which the four sons of Morgawse, Queen of Orkney, are
shown as being very badly brought up (unlike Arthur) by their mother.
Morgawse makes her first appearance boiling a cat (the way they
treat animals is always how we know what to think of people in T. H.
White), and is only interested in getting power over men, which is
why she turns up one day at Arthur's court and seduces him. Much
of this is very anti-Scottish – White seems to have a phobia about the
Scots and the Celts generally, and speaks at one point of 'the enormous, the incalculable miasma which is the leading feature of the
Gaelic brain' (p. 243), without apparently thinking that he is joking.
Interspersed with all this are the increasingly unfunny episodes of
comic relief in which King Pellinore continues to pursue the Questing
Beast.

The third book, *The Ill-Made Knight*, is about Lancelot, and concentrates on his unnatural purity – which enables him to cure people as
well as win fights – with the interesting innovation that he is very
ugly. The two major quests that he undertakes to escape the fatal
enervations of his love for Guenevere are close to Malory and contain
some of the best writing in the book. There are also embarrassing
reflections on the nature of love (inevitably Lancelot and Guenevere
fall in love 'with the click of two magnets coming together', p. 363)
and embarrassing conversations when Lancelot returns from his quests
and he and Guenevere start calling each other Jenny and Lance, and

talking about the things that Malory wisely avoided – what Guenevere said to Lancelot when he returned from seeing Elaine, or what Guenevere said to Elaine (White conflates Malory's Elaine, mother of Galahad, and Elaine of Astolat) when Elaine makes a visit to Camelot ('And how's the baby?' asks Guenevere, p. 393). But Malory always comes to White's rescue, and the scenes when Lancelot runs mad in the wood provide White with opportunities that he is much better at taking; so with Lancelot's return to Elaine, the nursing, the tournaments that are held to bring him back to his old self, where 'he just knocks everybody down who would stand up to him with a kind of absent-minded ferocity' and then wanders off disconsolate (p. 413). Meanwhile, baby Galahad is playing with a rag doll called 'the Holy Holy' (p. 414). Fifteen years pass, and Arthur introduces the Grail quest, from which Gawain, Lionel, Aglovale and finally Lancelot return, with their stories. There follow the three defences of Guenevere, where Meliagaunce, in a neat touch, is made into a common Cockney knight, and White shows his instinct for what is best in Malory's narrative by closing this book with the episode of the healing of Sir Urry.

The Candle in the Wind brings Mordred to the forefront of the story, opening with a revealing passage about his distaste for the smell of hawks. His conversations with Agravain show a couple of Machiavellian politicians at work, while the handling of the scenes with the other brothers is magnificent, especially the plotting to take Lancelot and Guenevere in the bedroom. Mordred uses Arthur's new rule of law cunningly, establishing a kind of popular party called the Thrashers who dress in black (presumably in allusion to the blackshirt fascists of pre–1939 Britain); he spreads anti-Arthurian propaganda, and the story moves to its great climax, following Malory now closely and gaining irresistible impetus from the wound-up spring of his narrative power.

White's novel is unanchored in any kind of historical reality, as is usual, but strangely full of historical references to the high Middle Ages. Uther Pendragon seems to merge with William the Conqueror, and seems to have reigned from 1066 to 1216. Robin Wood's men are Saxons who resist the Norman invasion (like Hereward the Wake). Arthur is Norman by origin and seems to rule over a Merrie England that runs indefinitely from 1216 and includes a reference to the John Ball who preached the Peasants' Revolt in 1381 though ending two

centuries before Malory wrote. This makes Arthur into all the Plan-
tagenet kings. White's description of Merrie England, in chapter 25 of
The Ill-Made Knight and again in chapter 3 of *Candle in the Wind*, is an
incredible historical goulash. Anyone who got their history here would
need their brains unscrambled.

There is much for the grown-up reader to dislike in White's books
– the cultivated quaintness, the conscious anachronism that he means
us to smile at and find charming (not ridiculous as in Twain), and the
whole world of prep schools and Oxford colleges that he evokes as
the points of reference for his idealized medieval world. The nurse of
the Castle of Foret Sauvage is like the matron or nurse of your old
preparatory school whose bark was worse than her bite, and the
Badger's sett is as cute as can be:

> Badger called it the Combination Room. All round the panelled room
> there were ancient paintings of departed badgers, famous in their day
> for scholarship and godliness, lit from above by shaded glowworms.
> (p. 189)

Lancelot is described as a sort of Bradman, top of the batting averages,
and Elaine has been following Lancelot's career like a schoolchild
doting on the batsman Hobbs. Cricket brings out the worst in White.
The eyes grow misty with nostalgia. . . . When Launcelot finds he has
been in bed with Elaine after being made drunk, he fears that he may
have lost his power as well as his virtue:

> Children believe such things to this day, and think they will only be
> able to bowl well in the cricket match tomorrow, provided that they are
> good today. (p. 376)

The oppressively avuncular and patronizing tone of such passages
seems not to bother younger readers.

The same tone creeps into White's psychological 'explanations',
again something he would have been wise to imitate Malory in avoiding. The Orkney brothers for instance have a problem because they
were deprived of the love of their mother, Agravain in particular
being terminally deranged because of his mother-fixation, while
Lancelot's urge to purity is because of something twisted and ugly
within him:

> Under the grotesque, magnificent shell with a face like Quasimodo's,
> there was shame and self-loathing which had been planted there when
> he was tiny, by something which it is now too late to trace. It is fatally
> easy to make children believe they are horrible. (p. 368)

It is even worse when explanations are hinted at that might be beyond younger readers – 'It's very difficult to explain about Guenevere's
love for two men at the same time' (p. 367); Guenevere is difficult to
write about because she is 'a real woman' (p. 472) – not a very
helpful remark to make in the middle of a book. Perhaps she loved
Arthur as a father and Lancelot because of the son she could not
have. But the account of Mordred has a weird power. It is not surprising he turned out badly, says White, considering that he knew his
father had sought his death, and that he had spent years alone with a
mother who hated his father –

> He was robbed of himself – his soul stolen, overlaid, wizened, while the
> mother-character lives in triumph, superfluously and with stifling love
> endowed on him, seemingly innocent of ill-intention. (pp. 611–12)

The influence here of White's own upbringing and his problems
with his own mother are only too painfully obvious, but they give an
authentic venom to his portrayal of Mordred. Arthur, by contrast,
was beautifully brought up, we are told (p. 388), by an elderly eccentric with no mother in sight – another advertisement for preparatory
schools and the peculiarly English habit of removing boys from their
native habitat at the age of seven and bringing them up to be terrified
of women.

But there are also some extraordinary strengths in White's work.
He can for instance be very informative about medieval practice if
not medieval history, particularly the practice of falconry, which he
returns to again and again, or the details and specifics of jousting.
There is a wonderful boar-hunt led by William Twyti, 'who almost
since he could remember had been either pursuing a hart or cutting
it up into helpings' (p. 142), and a dramatic realization of what a
cavalry charge of mounted knights really was like, at the battle of
Bedegraine (p. 300). Connected with this is White's perhaps special
gift, that imaginative inhabiting of other realms of experience, what it
is like to be a fish or a bird in its element. Birds bring out the best in

White: the story begins with the gripping account of Arthur trying to persuade the hawk Cully to return, and ends with the birds being blown about in the fierce wind that precedes the last battle. The scene of the praise of birds (p. 156), upon which Kay bursts with the news that he has just killed a thrush, is one of the finest passages in the book, surpassed only by the imagining of the world of the wild geese (p. 166). All these passages are in *The Sword in the Stone*. Of course, White would not be himself if he were not also teaching lessons in these passages. The pike in the castle moat teaches the lesson of power – 'There is nothing but power' (p. 52) – the geese teach the lesson of the unnaturalness of wars within a species, and the world of the ants teaches the dangers of the world in which the individual is subdued to the state. This is White's allegory of the creation of the communist state, against which he sets his vision of the ideal feudal order, his own cosy conservatism.

Following the long tradition in which Arthurian romance becomes the vehicle for a new age's ideology, White has a larger framework for his version of the Arthurian story, derived in a rather naive manner from Malory but not without its compelling power in driving the narrative onward. He traces a fourfold sequence.

Before Arthur there was lawless knight-errantry, in a country devastated by war, with no central administration or sense of nationhood, where the only law was 'Might is Right' (p. 225). Arthur must destroy that world in a new way, by total war, and at the battle of Bedegraine there are no ransoms, no leaving of all the dying to the hired soldiers, and no waiting about to start battles at the agreed hour. This is reminiscent of Twain's solution to the problem of the old order – dynamite it out of existence – though White has in mind (in memory, not in prospect) the idea of the First World War of 1914–18 as the war to end all wars, now overshadowed by the threat and soon the reality of the Second World War, which broke out in 1939 when White was in the midst of the original trilogy.

In the next stage, the Round Table is set up in order to channel the natural male tendency to violence into beneficial activities – Might in the service of Right. Lancelot is the exemplar of this order. But things start to go wrong with the Round Table: it turns into a kind of Games Mania, with people only doing what they do in order to improve their position in the league table of tilting averages, and soon the murderous feuds start up again. Understandably, White traces nothing of this to the disease of adultery; for him the enemy of the Round Table is an ineradicable strain of violence in men, particularly in the Scots brothers.

So Arthur thinks up a new idea, the quest for the Grail, which will direct all this male energy in a manner advantageous to the commonwealth. As Arthur says, preparing so to speak his term paper on Malory:

> I suppose that all endeavours which are directed to a purely worldly end, as my famous Civilization was, contain within themselves the germs of their own corruption. (p. 434)

But the knights return disillusioned, and the court enters its last phase (reminiscent of the world of Tennyson's 'The Last Tournament'), when it is 'modern' and fashionable, an indication of its corrupt, degraded and effeminate state being the long pointy shoes that men wear. White grows quite unhinged at the contemplation of his own modern age at the end of *The Ill-Made Knight*, using Malory's reflections on love then and love nowadays as a prompt for his own complainings about the new sexual permissiveness, in which 'adolescents pursue the ignoble spasms of the cinematograph' (p. 509). The introduction of Mordred at the beginning of *The Candle in the Wind*, published in 1958, sets White ranting again, this time in an extraordinary baleful account of the savagery and feral wit of the Gaels, the race now best represented by the Irish Republican Army (p. 518).

The final stage is the establishment of the rule of law – not Might is Right, nor Might for Right, nor Right is Might, but the abandonment of Might. Ironically, it is the manipulation of the law by Mordred that leads to the destruction of the Round Table. Arthur ends with some meditations on the subjects that preoccupied Twain: are men irredeemably wicked, or are they made so by wicked leaders, or do they simply get the leaders they deserve? The only thing he sees for certain is that everything is rooted in the past and that's why he sends Tom of Warwick (Malory was a 'Warwick man') off to tell the story. This is not at all a bad ending.

John Steinbeck, *The Acts of King Arthur and his Noble Knights*

Steinbeck's *Acts of King Arthur* was written 1958–9 but not published until 1976. The book started out as a retelling of Malory, but Steinbeck gradually succumbed to a disillusioned sense of the futility of chivalric story-telling and the translation ends prematurely when Lancelot and Guenevere, Hollywood-style, kiss for the first time.

Steinbeck, most famous for *The Grapes of Wrath* (1939), an eloquent indictment of oppressive labour practices against migrant workers in California during the depression of the 1930s, had a life-long passion for Malory, and in 1958, when he had settled down with his third wife (luckily called Elaine), he began his translation of Malory, which he regarded as the major project of his writing life. He says in his Introduction that his idea was to put Malory into 'plain present-day speech' so as to make it accessible to modern readers and get them away from 'comic-strip travesties'. His thinking about his boyhood experience of reading the book is admirably simple, and one can detect in it the familiar notion that the Arthurian story may provide a means to the redemption of a decayed modern age:

> I think my sense of right and wrong, my feeling of noblesse oblige, and any thought I may have against the oppressor and for the oppressed, came from this secret book. (p. xii)

What he managed to do during his year of work on the translation, during which time he was living with his wife in England at an idyllic country retreat in Somerset, was a series of stories extracted from Book I of Vinaver's edition of the Winchester manuscript, beginning with the birth of Arthur and the battle of Bedegraine and ending with the triple quest of Gawain, Ewain and Marhalt, and then, omitting Book II completely, a version of the tale of Sir Lancelot, Vinaver's Book III, ending with the first kiss of Lancelot and Guenevere ('Their bodies locked together as though a trap had sprung. Their mouths met and each devoured the other', p. 293), an episode which leaves one relieved he got no further. By October 1959 he had returned to New York, and no one ever saw another word of the translation.

What went wrong? The answer seems to be, as one starts to read, practically everything. One mistake is that he is always explaining things, and explaining them on the sort of level that might satisfy a nine-year-old. The explanation of Merlin's tricks is that 'he took joy in causing wonder' (p. 5) because he 'was aware that a simple open man is most receptive when he is mystified' (p. 4). There is nothing very wrong with explanations in themselves, but with this kind of story the more that is explained, the more inexplicable everything becomes, not mysteriously and wondrously inexplicable but irritatingly inexplicable. For instance, if the story of the sword in the stone is surrounded with circumstantial detail there is no possible reason why Arthur should not know what it is there for when he takes it out to give to Kay. He must be the only person in England who doesn't know by this point.

There is also the unfortunate accident that the parts Steinbeck started to work with were the parts where explanations were least convincing and hardest to come by and the parts that were the least amenable to any narrative gifts he could bring to them. They are deeply resistant to the novelist's desire to realize, dramatize, humanize, and as a result there is little imaginative absorption or transformation of the materials. The plain style meanwhile makes the material accessible in the wrong way, by removing the mystery which is intrinsic to Malory's style, and which both Twain and White, in their different ways, paid respect to (Twain by quoting Malory, White by using Malory's language as the dialect of High Chivalry in the land of 'Gramarye').

Another weakness is Steinbeck's proneness to cliché, to glib moralizations on almost any subject, something that was a weakness even in his best books – the tendency to think that it was the novelist's right to get up on the soapbox. 'Somewhere in the world there is defeat for everyone', says Merlin (p. 44), or, Merlin again, 'Misfortune is not fair, fate is not just, but they exist just the same' (p. 68) – large, empty, resoundingly hollow platitudes. 'In the combat between wisdom and feeling, wisdom never wins' (p. 99).

But a marked change comes over the retelling at the beginning of the story of the three quests. Steinbeck starts writing more in his own way: it's the moment that he alludes to in his letters when he realized that he had got to write in American (p. 325). The story begins to rattle along at a fair pace, with moments of commonplaceness and sentimentality and vulgarity but also with the love of and gift for story-telling that makes popular novelists popular. The story of Gawain and the youngest of the three damsels is very amusing – he thinking all the time that he's about to make an easy conquest, she scornful of the attentions of this woefully aged lover. The story of Marhalt and the thirty-year-old damsel becomes a kind of Hollywood-style camping trip, with the lady telling Marhalt to turn the other way while she changes into her spare underclothing (p. 158) and gradually behaving more and more like a nagging wife, telling Marhalt to tidy his things away and stop chewing on his moustache and change for dinner, so that Marhalt gradually goes off her. The great triumph of the book is the quest of Ewain and the older lady, who turns out to be an experienced semi-professional jousting coach and puts Ewain through a year's strenuous training. What is so good about this is not so much the relationship between the two, though this is well done, as the amount of interesting and practical detail Steinbeck is able to bring in about armour, weapons, horses and the technique of fighting on horseback. He sounds enormously knowledgeable, and the style acquires something of the zest of Hemingway's know-how writing. The description of the fight between Ewain and the twin-brother knights is technically one of the best in Arthurian literature.

The pace slackens with the beginning of the Lancelot story, and Steinbeck, finding himself becalmed, tries to get out of the doldrums with some execrably bad overwriting. The offer made to Lancelot by the Queen of North Galys, in a four-queen competition for his favours, of an endless life of intense sex, 'a crucifixion of love' (p. 236), is as embarrassing as could be.

A series of letters from Steinbeck to his agent and to his literary editor – a selection from which is printed in the Appendix to the Noonday edition – is interesting in tracing Steinbeck's preparation for and experience in writing his translation. He talks of his plans for the work, how it will be the greatest work he has undertaken, and of the vast amounts of research and travelling he is doing to prepare for his mission. His research usually consists of asking his agent to send him books on the Middle Ages, from which he proceeds to concoct the craziest theories. He debates with himself whether he is justified in doing his translation in modern English, but decides that since that is what Malory was doing in his day (wrong), there is no reason why he should not do the same. But he keeps talking about what he's going to do, never doing anything, making plans, doing nothing, doing research, going to Italy to do research (a more research-proof escape plan could hardly be imagined), finding what he writes 'missing on several cylinders', and becoming dissatisfied because he feels his writing has become too glib. But when he went to live in Somerset in March 1959, everything started to go right, and the words began to flow. There's a lot of complaining about the 'terrible mess' that Malory presents him with and how he has to keep disentangling the story from the undergrowth of digression and leading the story to a proper climax, though constantly with the sense that he is doing what Malory would have himself wanted to do if he could. 'I think it is good writing – as good in its way as Malory's was in its way: I am awfully excited about it' (pp. 336–7).

Then there came a terrible blow. In May 1959 his New York agent and editor wrote to him and seem to have conveyed that they were disappointed with what he had sent them. Steinbeck was devastated; he tried to explain that they had not really understood what he was trying to do, that he had read T. H. White (which they had obviously mentioned as a possible model) and thought it was good, but he was not trying to do the same thing. He tried to recover his enthusiasm, but he was now finding more and more to complain about in Malory – the shadowy role of Arthur, who turns out to be 'a dope', the ridiculousness of the stories:

> As I go along, I am constantly jiggled by the arrant nonsense of a great deal of the material. A great deal of it makes no sense at all. Two thirds of it is the vain dreaming of children talking in the dark. (p. 349)

But then he throws caution to the winds and just gets going in his own way with the Triple Quest:

> I have a feeling that I am really rolling now in the stories of Ewain, Gawain and Marhalt. In the first place it is a better story and in the second I am trying to open it out. Where Malory plants an incident and then forgets it, I pick it up. (p. 350)

He becomes more and more cavalier in his remarks about Malory:

> Difficulty with work today. . . . That damned Malory has got this quest in his teeth and is running mad with fighting. Also he gets so excited about curing crowds with a piece of bloody cloth that he gets all mixed up about who and why. Then he has Lancelot masquerading in Sir Kay's armor and suddenly forgets all about it. And I have to excavate these things and give them some point or else cut them out. (p. 356)

He is not going to give Lancelot any adventures unless they have a point, he says, or contribute to the development of the plot.

But by August 1959 he was totally dissatisfied with the whole thing, dissatisfied with Somerset – after all, he says, the room where you write is just the room where you write, and it doesn't matter where it is – dissatisfied with England. By October he was back in New York and he said no more about the book for six years. On 8 July 1965 he wrote:

> I go struggling along with the matter of Arthur. I think I have some-thing and I am pretty excited about it. (p. 364)

I think everyone who has tried to write, at any level, will recognize the pathos of that – 'I am pretty excited about it'.

The Modern Arthur: Novels and Films

The forms of modern fantasy which Arthurian romance has fed in modern novels, films and television adaptations are steeped, as always, in the manner to which we have grown accustomed, in the cultural issues and debates of their time. A feminist slant is given in Bradley's *The Mists of Avalon*; the quest for the Grail becomes both an image for the inspiring power of idealism (in the film of *The Fisher King*) and also a lesson in the disasters to which idealism may lead. Arthurian stories are also appropriated to the crassest Hollywood sentimentalities, as in the film called *First Knight* (1998), where the story of Lancelot and Guenevere is given a happy ending.

There was some continuation, in the twentieth century, of the Victorian tradition of verse narrative on Arthurian themes. John Masefield wrote a cycle of Arthurian poems, and the American poet Edward Arlington Robinson wrote an Arthurian trilogy in blank verse (*Merlin*, 1917; *Lancelot*, 1920; *Tristram*, 1927). In *Tristram*, as in Matthew Arnold's poem, the sympathy is all with the stoic love and endurance of Iseult of Brittany. The poems of Charles Williams, *Taliessin through Logres* (1938) and *The Region of the Summer Stars* (1944), are reworkings of Arthurian themes to fit quasi-mystical religious ideas expounded by C. S. Lewis in *Arthurian Torso*, which was published with Williams's poems in 1974.

But the bulk of modern Arthurian writing has been in the form of the novel, as in T. H. White and (putatively) John Steinbeck, and particularly in novels for younger readers. Rosemary Sutcliff has *The Lantern Bearers* (1959) and *Sword at Sunset* (1963), and four further Arthurian books for children; in *Firelord* (1980), by Parke Godwin, Arthur dictates his memoirs; Marion Zimmer Bradley, in her influential novel *The Mists of Avalon* (1982), tells Arthur's story through the eyes of the women who were involved in it, especially Ygraine. There are other novels, usually superior as novels, which do not tell the Arthurian story but are inspired by elements in it. In *The Natural* (1952), by Bernard Malamud, the hero (Roy) is a naive country lad (like Perceval) who has a wondrous baseball bat (sword) and comes to the aid of a baseball team called the New York Knights (managed by Pop Fisher) whose play prior to his arrival has been, so to speak, impotent. Roy, like Perceval, just wants to be 'the best there ever was in the game' (and learns of course that there is more to the game than that). In *Lancelot* (1978), by Walker Percy, a southern lawyer called Lancelot Laman, bitter and impotent, tries to prove his wife's infidelity by filming it, and ends up in a madhouse, whence he tells his story. The characters of David Lodge's *Small World* (1984) are constantly discussing the Grail, and the elderly and impotent patriarch of the literary establishment, Arthur Kingfisher, is cured at a New York meeting of the Modern Language Association when Persse asks the right question. *Lance*, a short story by Vladimir Nabokov, is an interpretative quagmire. There are many other Arthurian novels, and of course Arthurian themes have a vigorous life in comics.

As to the cinema, there are over forty full-length Arthurian feature films to date, some of them well worth forgetting, like *The Black Knight* (1954), with Alan Ladd, or *Sword of the Valiant* (1984), the story of *Sir Gawain and the Green Knight*, with Sean Connery as the Green Knight. *A Connecticut Yankee in King Arthur's Court* (1949) is a toothless version of Twain's novel, with Bing Crosby and Rhonda Fleming, and Sir Cedric Hardwicke as a doddery King Arthur. *The Knights of the Round Table* (1953), with Robert Taylor as Lancelot and Ava Gardner as Guenevere, tells the story of Lancelot's return from exile to defeat Mordred. *The Sword in the Stone* (1963) is a Walt Disney film based on T. H. White, concentrating mostly on the early scenes between Merlin and Wart. *Camelot* (1967) is a version of the Broadway musical of 1960 with music by Frederick Loewe and words by Alan Jay Lerner. It is based on T. H. White, stars Richard Harris and Vanessa Redgrave, and is one of the happier Arthurian cinematic confections. The *Gawain and the Green Knight* of 1972, which has little relation to the medieval poem, is still a good deal better than *Sword of the Valiant*, which has less. Robert Bresson's *Lancelot du Lac* (1974) is a darkly atmospheric evocation of the story of the doomed lovers, with much gloomy clangour of ironmongery. *Monty Python and the Holy Grail* (1975) is an inspired take-off of a remarkable number of Arthurian themes, with moments of parodic brilliance that provide some of the best arguments for reading Arthurian romance and by that means getting to know more fully what is being sent up. *Perceval le Gallois* (1978), directed by Eric Rohmer, is based directly on Chrétien de Troyes, with much medievalization in the design of the film. *Excalibur* (1981), directed by John Boorman, is the definitive Arthurian movie. With the help of T. H. White, and a bewilderingly eccentric performance by Nicol Williamson as Merlin, it attempts to tell the whole story. It has many flaws, but it could have been far worse.

Norris Lacy, in an essay on Arthurian films, comments on the tyranny of tradition.[1] The reasons for making such films, he points out, are usually to cash in on the popularity of the name and story (which is largely because it involves sex and violence), and this means that the audience expects certain 'canonical' elements. So there is a conflict between the film-makers' desire to innovate and respond freshly to the story and the anxiety to be close to what the audience knows. This is one reason, it might be added, why the best 'Arthurian' films are those that are 'inspired by' rather than retell Arthurian stories. In *Knightriders* (1981), directed by George Romero, motorcycle riders travel around the country and present Arthurian 'tournaments'; they too, like the knights of the Round Table, have their problems. It is an Arthurian biker film – but the story from the start is always being modernized, treated as a live legend, not an antique. *The Natural* (1984) is basically a good film of Malamud's novel, but some of the subtleties of Arthurian allusion are lost in the process of adaptation for a more general audience. *The Fisher King* (1991), directed by Terry Gilliam, with its elusive Grail and sad evocation of the Waste Land in low-life Manhattan, is beautifully tangential to Arthurian interests.

There are and will be many other Arthurian films, and already too many television adaptations.

Notes

Chapter 1: The Early Arthur

1 Simon Martin and Nikolai Grube, *Chronicle of the Maya Kings and Queens* (London: Thames and Hudson, 2001). The review is in the *Times Literary Supplement*, 24 August 2001.
2 Winston S. Churchill, *A History of the English-speaking Peoples*, 4 vols (London: Cassell, 1956–8), vol. 1, p. 47.
3 Martin B. Shichtmann and James P. Carley (eds), *Culture and the King: The Social Implications of the Arthurian Legend* (Albany: State University of New York Press, 1994), Introduction, p. 4.
4 There is an illustration of the archivolt in Roger Sherman Loomis (ed.), *Arthurian Literature in the Middle Ages: A Collaborative History* (Oxford: Clarendon Press, 1959), at p. 60.
5 Agnellus of Ravenna, *Liber pontificalis ecclesiae Ravennae*, cited and translated by Charles Jones, *Saints' Lives and Chronicles in Early England* (Ithaca, New York: Cornell University Press, 1947), p. 63.
6 Layamon's name is correctly spelt 'Laʒamon', with 'ʒ' (called 'yogh') standing for the sound that is now represented by 'w' (his name therefore means 'lawman'). 'Layamon' is commonly used for convenience.

Chapter 2: The Romancing of the Arthurian Story: Chrétien de Troyes

1 Erich Auerbach, *Mimesis: The Representation of Reality in Western Literature* (1946; translated by Willard R. Trask, 1953; Princeton, New Jersey: Princeton University Press, 1957), p. 118.
2 Stephen Knight, *Arthurian Literature and Society* (London: Macmillan, 1983), pp. xiv–xv.

3 Ibid., pp. 76–7, citing Georges Duby, 'Youth in Aristocratic Society', in *The Chivalrous Society* (London: Arnold, 1977).

4 Rosalind Field, 'The Anglo-Norman Background to Alliterative Romance', in D. A. Lawton (ed.), *Middle English Alliterative Poetry and its Literary Background: Seven Essays* (Cambridge: D. S. Brewer, 1982), pp. 54–69 (see pp. 64–5).

5 Knight, *Arthurian Literature and Society*, p. 85.

6 See Donald Maddox, 'Lévi-Strauss in Camelot: Interrupted Communication in Arthurian Fiction', in Shichtmann and Carley (eds), *Culture and the King*, pp. 35–53 (p. 37).

7 Jean Frappier, 'Chrétien de Troyes', in Loomis (ed.), *Arthurian Literature in the Middle Ages*, pp. 157–91 (p. 164).

Chapter 3: The European Flourishing of Arthurian Romance: Lancelot, Parzival, Tristan

1 See Keith Busby, *Gauvain in Old French Literature* (Amsterdam: Rodopi, 1980), p. 252.

2 Jessie L. Weston, *From Ritual to Romance* (Cambridge: Cambridge University Press, 1920); T. S. Eliot, *The Waste Land* (1922).

3 Jean Frappier, 'The Vulgate Cycle', in Loomis (ed.), *Arthurian Literature in the Middle Ages*, pp. 295–318 (quotation at pp. 298–9).

4 The vocabulary here is appropriated from Malory: it is not untrue to the formal manner of the French prose romances, though there is something also, it must be admitted, finding its way in from Mark Twain.

5 Jean Frappier, 'The Vulgate Cycle', p. 316.

6 Dante, *The Divine Comedy, Inferno*, V.127–38 ('. . . they read no more that day').

7 Novalis (pseudonym of Friedrich Hardenberg, the German romantic writer), cited in Denis de Rougemont, *Passion and Society* (London: Faber, 1940; revised edition, 1956), p. 219.

Chapter 4: Arthur, Lancelot and Gawain in Ricardian England

1 See especially William Matthews, *The Tragedy of Arthur: A Study of the Alliterative 'Morte Arthure'* (Berkeley: University of California Press, 1960).

2 Lee Patterson, 'The Romance of History and the Alliterative *Morte Arthure*', *Journal of Medieval and Renaissance Studies*, 13 (1983), reprinted in revised form as chapter 6 in his *Negotiating the Past: The Historical Understanding of Medieval Literature* (Madison: University of Wisconsin Press, 1987), pp. 197–230, which is cited here.

3   W. P. Ker, *Epic and Romance: Essays on Medieval Literature* (1896; New York: Dover Publications, 1957), p. 335.

4   J. A. Burrow, 'Honour and Shame in *Sir Gawain and the Green Knight*', in his *Essays on Medieval Literature* (Oxford: Clarendon Press, 1984), pp. 117–31 (p. 126).

5   A. C. Spearing, *The Gawain-Poet: A Critical Study* (Cambridge: Cambridge University Press, 1970), p. 226.

6   William Ian Miller, a scholar of Icelandic literature and law, argues that humiliation, shame and embarrassment are 'the central emotions of everyday social existence', and quotes the view of the philosopher Richard Rorty that 'the humiliatibility of human kind' is a social-psychological universal that transcends differences between cultures: see *Humiliation and Other Essays on Honour, Social Discomfort and Violence* (Ithaca, New York: Cornell University Press, 1993). In a discussion of *Sir Gawain and the Green Knight* Miller argues that 'shame' was once used to cover much of the ground now assigned to 'embarrassment' and 'humiliation' – the words did not exist, but the feelings did, and the poet of *Gawain* knew about them.

Chapter 5: Malory's *Morte D'Arthur*

1   For an excellent account of the *Morte D'Arthur* in these terms, see Jill Mann, *The Narrative of Distance, The Distance of Narrative in Malory's 'Morte DArthur'*, The William Matthews Lectures (University of London, Birkbeck College, 1991). See also her earlier essay, 'Taking the Adventure: Malory and the *Suite du Merlin*', in Derek Brewer and Toshiyuki Takamiya (eds), *Aspects of Malory* (*Arthurian Studies*, 1) (Cambridge: D. S. Brewer, 1981), pp. 71–91.

2   See A. B. Ferguson, *The Indian Summer of English Chivalry* (Durham, North Carolina: Duke University Press, 1960).

3   C. S. Lewis, 'The English Prose *Morte*', in J. A. W. Bennett (ed.), *Essays on Malory* (Oxford: Clarendon Press, 1963), pp. 7–28 (p. 10).

4   These are the terms used by Knight, *Arthurian Literature and Society*, pp. 112, 114.

5   For a description of the action of romance-narrative as 'a kind of balletic realisation of important aspects of experience', see Mann, *Narrative of Distance*, p. 7.

6   Terence McCarthy, '*Le Morte Darthur* and Romance,' in Derek Brewer (ed.), *Studies in Medieval English Romances: Some New Approaches* (Cambridge: D. S. Brewer, 1988), pp. 148–75 (p. 172).

Chapter 6: The Arthurian Sleep and the Romantic Revival: Tennyson's *Idylls of the King*

1 See James Douglas Merriman, *The Flower of Kings: A Study of Arthurian Legend in England between 1485 and 1835* (Lawrence, Kansas: University Press of Kansas, 1973), p. 47. Merriman's book is in all respects an excellent guide to the period covered by the present chapter.

2 Roberta Florence Brinkley, *The Arthurian Legend in the Seventeenth Century*, Johns Hopkins Monographs in Literary History, vol. 3 (Baltimore, 1932), pp. 9–10. Brinkley's book provides much of the material for this section; also Merriman, *Flower of Kings*, pp. 49–72.

3 See David R. Carlson, 'Arthur Before and After the Revolution: The Blome-Stansby Edition of Malory (1634) and *Brittains Glory* (1684)', in Shichtmann and Carley (eds), *Culture and the King*, pp. 234–53. Carlson reproduces the woodcut at p. 236.

4 Merriman, *Flower of Kings*, p. 62.

5 Voltaire's *Essai sur les moeurs* and Hume's *History of England* are cited thus in Merriman, *Flower of Kings*, p. 74.

6 This is the title of a book by Mark Girouard, *The Return to Camelot: Chivalry and the English Gentleman* (New Haven, Connecticut: Yale University Press, 1981), which provides material for the next paragraphs.

7 'Idylls' was pronounced by Tennyson 'idles' (as also in the United States today).

8 This is the American writer U. W. Cutler, in 1905, as cited in Girouard, *Return to Camelot*, the source for much of the information in this paragraph.

Chapter 7: Mark Twain, T. H. White, John Steinbeck and the Modern Arthur

1 Norris Lacy, 'Arthurian Film and the Tyranny of Tradition', *Arthurian Interpretations*, 4 (1989), pp. 75–85.

Bibliography of Works Cited and Further Reading

Editions Used

The following editions are used in this book for citation and reference. They are listed here in the order in which they appear, chapter by chapter.

Chapter 1: The Early Arthur

Gildas, *The Ruin of Britain*, edited and translated by Michael Winterbottom (Chichester: Phillimore, 1978).

Geoffrey of Monmouth, *The History of the Kings of Britain*, translated by Lewis Thorpe (Harmondsworth: Penguin, 1966).

Arthurian Chronicles, represented by Wace and Layamon, translated by Eugene Mason (London: J. M. Dent, 1912). This translation, in which any delicacy of flavour in the original is likely to be swamped in a surfeit of false archaism of the 'Friend, tarry here no further, whomsoever thou mayst be' (p. 83) kind, is occasionally emended.

Layamon's *Brut*. There is an edition of the whole of the *Brut* (over 16,000 long lines in the more complete of the two manuscripts in which it survives) by G. L. Brook and R. F. Leslie, 2 vols, Early English Text Society, 250, 277 (London: Oxford University Press, 1963, 1978). The Arthurian sections (lines 9229–14297) are edited with a facing-page translation into modern English by W. R. J. Barron and S. C. Weinberg in *Laȝamon's Arthur* (Austin: University of Texas Press, 1989).

Chapter 2: The Romancing of the Arthurian Story: Chrétien de Troyes

Chrétien de Troyes, *Arthurian Romances*, translated by William W. Kibler and Carleton W. Carroll (London: Penguin, 1991).

Chapter 3: The European Flourishing of Arthurian Romance: Lancelot, Parzival, Tristan

The 'Vulgate cycle' of French prose Arthurian romances is edited by H. O. Sommer, 8 vols (1909–13, with Index added 1916). Volume 1 contains the *Estoire del Saint Graal*, volume 2 the *Merlin*, volumes 3–5 the *Lancelot*, volume 6 the *Queste del Saint Graal* and the *Mort Artu*, and volume 7 the *Livre d'Artus* (a later eclectic compilation which Sommer supposed to be one of the building blocks of the Vulgate cycle). The more modern edition of the *Lancelot* by Alexandre Micha (Geneva: Librairie Droz, 1978–82) covers the contents only of volume 4 of Sommer's edition and itself occupies eight volumes.

Gottfried von Strassburg, *Tristan und Isolt*, edited by August Closs (Oxford: Blackwell, 1947).

Gottfried von Strassburg, *Tristan* (with the *Tristran* of Thomas), translated by A. T. Hatto (Harmondsworth: Penguin, 1960).

Chapter 4: Arthur, Lancelot and Gawain in Ricardian England

Geoffrey Chaucer, *The Canterbury Tales*, in Larry D. Benson (ed.), *The Riverside Chaucer* (Boston: Houghton Mifflin, 1987).

Ywain and Gawain, edited by A. B. Friedman and N. T. Harrington, Early English Text Society, Original Series 254 (London: Oxford University Press, 1964).

Text of both the alliterative *Morte Arthure* and the stanzaic *Morte Arthur* is taken from the edition of the two poems in *King Arthur's Death*, edited by Larry D. Benson (Indianapolis and New York: Bobbs-Merrill, 1974), where the spelling is regularized according to a Middle English standard. There is a modern English verse translation of both poems, by Brian Stone, in *King Arthur's Death: Morte Arthure, Le Morte Arthur* (London: Penguin, 1988).

There are many editions and translations of *Sir Gawain and the Green Knight*. The edition used here (in which there is some modernization of spelling) is that of J. A. Burrow (London: Penguin, 1972).

Chapter 5: Malory's *Morte D'Arthur*

Text of Malory's *Morte D'Arthur* is taken from the modernized version (somewhat abridged) of the Winchester manuscript of the *Morte* edited by Helen

Cooper (Oxford: Oxford University Press, 1998). Passages omitted from this edition are cited from the modernized version of Caxton's print of *Le Morte D'Arthur* edited by Janet Cowen, 2 vols (Harmondsworth: Penguin, 1969). Cowen's edition (pp. 3–7) is also used for Caxton's Preface. The standard text of the Winchester manuscript, in original spelling, is that of Eugène Vinaver: Malory, *Works* (Oxford: Oxford University Press, 1971; 2nd edition, 1977). Both editions of the Winchester manuscript give marginal cross-references to the books and chapters of Caxton's print, and these are the references used in the text here.

Chapter 6: The Arthurian Sleep and the Romantic Revival: Tennyson's *Idylls of the King*

Roger Ascham, *The Scholemaster*, edited by John Daye (1570), as reprinted in Ascham's *English Works*, edited by W. A. Wright (Cambridge: Cambridge University Press, 1904).

The Poetical Works of Edmund Spenser, edited by J. C. Smith and E. de Selincourt (Oxford: Oxford University Press, 1912).

John Milton is cited from the 18-volume Columbia University edition of the *Complete Works* (1931–2), general editor F. A. Patterson. The *History of Britain* is in volume 10, *Paradise Lost* in volume 2, part 1, and *Paradise Regained* in volume 2, part 2.

Tom Thumb the Great, in *The Works of Henry Fielding* (London: Smith, Elder and Co., 1882), vol. 8.

The Poetical Works of Sir Walter Scott (London: Adam and Charles Black, 1880).

Alfred Lord Tennyson, *The Idylls of the King*, edited by J. M. Gray (London: Penguin, 1983).

Chapter 7: Mark Twain, T. H. White, John Steinbeck and the Modern Arthur

Mark Twain, *A Connecticut Yankee in King Arthur's Court*, edited by Bernard L. Stein, The Mark Twain Library (Berkeley and Los Angeles: University of California Press, 1979).

T. H. White, *The Once and Future King* (New York: Ace Books, 1987).

John Steinbeck, *The Acts of King Arthur and his Noble Knights, from the Winchester MSS.* [*sic*] *of Thomas Malory and other Sources*, edited by Chase Horton (New York: Noonday Press, Farrar, Straus and Giroux, 1976). This edition also includes a selection of Steinbeck's letters on the subject of his translation.

Further Reading

Archibald, Elizabeth, and A. S. G. Edwards (eds), *A Companion to Malory* (*Arthurian Studies*, 37) (Cambridge: D. S. Brewer, 1996).

Barber, Richard W., *King Arthur: Hero and Legend* (Woodbridge: Boydell and Brewer, 1986).

Barron, W. R. J. (ed.), *The Arthur of the English: The Arthurian Legend in Medieval English Life and Literature* (Cardiff: University of Wales Press, 2001).

Baswell, Christopher, and William Sharpe (eds), *The Passing of Arthur: New Essays on the Arthurian Tradition* (New York: Garland Press, 1988).

Braswell, Mary Flowers, and John Bugge (eds), *The Arthurian Tradition: Essays in Convergence* (Tuscaloosa: University of Alabama Press, 1988).

Brinkley, Roberta Florence, *The Arthurian Legend in the Seventeenth Century*, Johns Hopkins Monographs in Literary History, vol. 3 (Baltimore, 1932).

Busby, Keith (ed.), *Word and Image in Arthurian Literature* (New York: Garland Press, 1996).

Girouard, Mark, *The Return to Camelot: Chivalry and the English Gentleman* (New Haven, Connecticut: Yale University Press, 1981).

Harty, Kevin J., *Cinema Arthuriana* (New York: Garland Press, 1992).

Knight, Stephen, *Arthurian Literature and Society* (London: Macmillan, 1983).

Lacy, Norris J., and Geoffrey Ashe, *The New Arthurian Encyclopaedia*, revised edition (New York: Garland Press, 1996).

Lacy, Norris J., Geoffrey Ashe and Debra N. Mancoff (eds), *The Arthurian Handbook*, 2nd edition (New York: Garland Press, 1997).

Lagorio, Valerie, and Mildred Leake Day (eds), *King Arthur through the Ages*, 2 vols (New York: Garland Press, 1990).

Loomis, Roger Sherman, *Arthurian Legends in Medieval Art* (New York: MLA Press, 1938).

Loomis, Roger Sherman (ed.), *Arthurian Literature in the Middle Ages: A Collaborative History* (Oxford: Clarendon Press, 1959).

Lupack, Alan (ed.), *New Directions in Arthurian Studies* (Cambridge: D. S. Brewer, 2002).

Lupack, Alan, and Barbara Tepa Lupack, *King Arthur in America* (*Arthurian Studies*, 41) (Rochester, New York: D. S. Brewer, 1999).

Mancoff, Debra N., *The Return of King Arthur: The Legend through Victorian Eyes* (New York: Abrams, 1995).

Merriman, James Douglas, *The Flower of Kings: A Study of Arthurian Legend in England between 1485 and 1835* (Lawrence, Kansas: University Press of Kansas, 1973).

Poulson, Christine, *The Quest for the Grail: Arthurian Legend in British Art 1840– 1920* (Manchester: Manchester University Press, 1999).

Shichtmann, Martin B., and James P. Carley (eds), *Culture and the King: The Social Implications of the Arthurian Legend* (Albany: State University of New York Press, 1994).

Simpson, Roger, *Camelot Regained: The Arthurian Revival and Tennyson, 1800–1849* (Cambridge: D. S. Brewer, 1990).

Taylor, Beverly, and Elizabeth Brewer, *The Return of King Arthur: British and American Arthurian Literature since 1800* (Cambridge: D. S. Brewer, 1983).

Umland, Rebecca A., and Samuel J. Umland, *The Use of Arthurian Legend in Hollywood Film: From Connecticut Yankees to Fisher Kings* (Westport, Connecticut: Greenwood Press, 1996).

Whitaker, Muriel, *The Legends of King Arthur in Art* (Cambridge: D. S. Brewer, 1995).

There are two journals devoted to Arthurian studies, *Arthuriana* and *Arthurian Interpretations*, and a series, *Arthurian Studies*, published by D. S. Brewer.

Index

Height: 68
Bust added in.: 78